F
STRELECKY

Return to The Why Café

Other Works by **John P. Strelecky**

The Why Café

Life Safari

The Big Five for Life

How to be Rich and Happy (co-author)

The Mommy Butterfly and the Baby Egg (children's book)

RETURN TO THE WHY CAFÉ

∽

JOHN P. STRELECKY

Aspen Light Publishing

Many of the designations used by manufacturers and sellers to distinguish their products are claimed as trademarks. Where those designations appear in this book and Aspen Light Publishing was aware of a trademark claim, those designations have been printed with initial capital letters.

Copyright © 2014 by John P. Strelecky

All rights reserved. No part of this publication may be reproduced, stored in a retrieval system, or transmitted, in any form or by any means, electronic, mechanical, photocopying, recording, or otherwise, without the prior written permission of the publisher.

Printed in the United States of America.

Publication Data
Strelecky, John P.
Return to The Why Café / John P. Strelecky. — 1st Aspen Light Publishing ed.

ISBN-13: 978-0-991-39201-8

Published by Aspen Light Publishing

Inquiries to the author can be directed to:
John P. Strelecky c/o Aspen Light Publishing
13506 Summerport Village Parkway Suite #155
Windermere, FL 34786

The author can be reached through
www.whycafe.com

⁀ Prologue

Sometimes when you least expect it, and perhaps most need it, you find yourself in a new place, with new people, and you learn new things. That happened to me one night many years ago at a little place known affectionately as—*The Why Café*.

My night there set my life on a path I had never imagined. I learned about true freedom and came to realize that was my calling.

I never knew how or why I got to visit the café when I did. I was just grateful for the chance.

Then one day, under the most unlikely of circumstances, I found myself in front of the café once again. And once more, my time there changed my life in a direction for which I will forever be grateful.

This is the story of my return to—*The Why Café*.

∽ Chapter 1

It was a perfect day. The sky was a majestic blue, the air was warm but not oppressive. I felt like I was in paradise. Which I sort of was. Hawaii has that feel to it.

My entire plan for the day consisted of going for a bike ride. That was it. No schedule, no pre-arranged route, no agenda. Just a long ride, pedaling along random roads, going where my intuition guided me. Just me, my bike, and paradise to explore.

I'd been at it for a couple of hours and now had no clue where I was. Which was exactly what I wanted.

One of my favorite songs flashed through my mind. It's by an artist named Jana Stanfield. The lyrics are, "I am not lost, I am exploring." That fit my ride perfectly. In many respects, it fit most of my adventures perfectly.

Suddenly, my mind flashed back to a random night many years earlier. Only that time I hadn't felt like I was exploring. I'd just felt lost. It was a night which changed my life. A night spent at a little place called— The Why Are You Here Café. Known affectionately by those who visit, as The Why Café.

So much had changed since that night. It was almost hard to remember my life back then. It felt like another existence. Another me.

I cruised around a curve in the road and caught a glimpse of the ocean. So incredibly blue. I thought of a sea turtle. Another connection to that night at the café.

It was strange. The café never really left me. I hadn't had it flash through my thoughts with this intensity in a long time though.

Two more turns of the road. Two more spectacular views.

Hawaii has this incredible mix of colors. Since the islands were formed from volcanoes, they have deep black lava rock everywhere. Then, as if nature wanted to provide the perfect contrast, as the lava rock breaks down, the most vibrant green plants grown in the new soil. Add in the turquoise blue of the ocean waters and a myriad of oranges, reds, and other brilliant colors from the array of flowers everywhere...and it's an incredible treat for the eyes.

"Amazing," I thought to myself. "So amazing."

My last ten months had been full of *amazing*. Watching whales off the coast of South Africa, going on safari in Namibia, helping hatchling sea turtles escape into the surf in Central America. My trip had culminated with a three month bike adventure through Malaysia and Indonesia. Now, as I was heading home, I'd stopped off for a few extra weeks in Hawaii.

After all, when you're that close to paradise...might as well play there for a while.

This wasn't my first foray into exploring the world. After my night in the café long ago, I'd adopted a new approach to life. I work for a year, then travel for a year. Work for another year, then travel for another year. It seems strange to most people. They're worried about security and safety. It works for me though. I've found that when you're good at what you do, you're always in demand. Getting a new job has never been a problem.

The same people who have found my life strange, often tell me they'd love to try what I do. With rare exception, none of them has though. Even the ones who've said how much fun it would be to meet up with me for just a couple of weeks—never have.

I guess it's too much of a leap into the unknown.

More pedaling. More incredible views. The air was sweet with the scent of flowers. One of the things I love about Hawaii is the smell of the flowers. It's like breathing in nectar. Nature at its most pure.

Another two miles and I was in a section of the island I'd never visited before. It was flatter here. I could hear the surf off to my right. There was a fork in the road. Go right or go left.

"Take the road less traveled," I thought. "Always the one less traveled." That was the one on the right. I took it. The pavement gave way to gravel and I could feel my muscles straining with the new challenge. I liked that feeling—whether it was my mind, my legs, or some other muscle. That's when I knew I was on an adventure. When there was something new, something exciting, something that pushed me.

As I biked, I caught glimpses of the water through the trees. "Maybe I'll go for a swim later," I thought.

After about twenty minutes of pedaling on the gravel road, I suddenly felt a strange sense of deja vu. It was odd. I'd definitely never been to this part of the island before. Yet somehow....

I was just trying to sort through that feeling, when I saw it. Slightly farther up the road, on the right. A little white building, with a gravel parking lot in front, and a blue neon sign on the top.

I almost fell off my bike. "Impossible," I thought. But of course nothing is impossible—at The Why Café.

I rode closer and a smile came across my face. So many memories. So many insights that had been gained in that place. But what was the café doing here? Now? This was definitely not where I'd found it before.

I glanced behind me. There was no one, so I pushed hard on the pedals and increased my speed. I wanted to get to the café, so it couldn't disappear before I had a chance to go inside.

I needn't have worried. In five minutes I was there and it was still there too. My eyes took it in. "I can't believe it," I said.

There was a bike rack near the front door and I put my bike in it. My mind was alive with interest. *What was the café doing here?*

⁕ Chapter 2

I quickly climbed the front steps and after a moment of hesitation, pulled open the door to the café. There were bells on the door. The same bells as last time. They rang to announce my arrival.

I stepped inside and looked around. It was like stepping back in time. It looked *exactly* like when I'd been there almost ten years earlier. The red booths, the silver stools, the breakfast counter.... And it all still looked brand new.

"Welcome back, John."

I turned to my left. A moment before there had been no one. Now there was. It was Casey, the waitress who had waited on me when I'd visited the café before. I'd spent the entire night talking to her, the owner of the café and a customer. It was their concepts and ideas which had changed my life.

Casey was smiling.

I smiled back, "Hi, Casey."

She came toward me and gave me a warm hug. "It's been a while."

I nodded, still amazed at where I was and now who I was speaking with. "You look great," I said. "You look... the same." It was true. She hadn't aged at all.

She smiled again, "You look good too, John."

I looked around the café. "I can't believe I'm here. The café was on my mind this morning, really strongly. But to find it here...."

"We move around sometimes," she said. As if that perfectly explained how the identical café I'd visited years earlier was now in a location thousands of miles from where I'd originally visited it. Not to mention it looked like it hadn't changed at all.

"Or maybe we're franchising," she said and smiled again.

I laughed. She was kidding me because of a comment I'd made last time at the café. How did she remember that?

She motioned toward a booth, "Care to sit?"

I slid in, running my hands over the seats. They felt totally new.

"Can I get you something?" Casey asked and put a menu on the table.

I smiled. I remembered the menu. The one with the magic text which appeared and disappeared. I picked it up.

The last time I'd visited the café, there were three questions on the back of the menu.

Why are you here?

Do you fear death?

Are you fulfilled?

I turned the menu over. There they were. Oh how my life had changed because of those three questions.

"Things are a little different for you now. Aren't they?" Casey asked.

I looked up at her and smiled. "They are. Very different. In very good ways."

"Such as?"

I shook my head. "Wow, where would I start?"

Casey slid into the booth opposite me. She reached out and covered my hand with hers. "How about the morning you left the café ten years ago?"

◌◌ Chapter 3

I turned my hand and gently squeezed Casey's. It was warm. She was real. I really was back at the café.

I shook my head a little in disbelief and then smiled. "Well, let's see," I began. "Armed with the café menu you gave me, a piece of Mike's strawberry-rhubarb pie, and pretty much an entirely new perspective about life, I walked out of this place last time and into a whole new reality.

"That night changed me. To this day, what I learned still ripples through so many aspects of my life. The green sea turtle story, the fisherman story, talking with Anne about being the one who chooses my own version of reality.... It's all such a big part of the way I live my life now."

Casey smiled and leaned back in her seat. She nodded toward the café entrance, "You weren't so happy the last time you walked in that door."

I smiled back, "It's better now. As a matter of fact, it's so much better I have a tough time remembering what my life used to be like. I mean I really have to think hard to remember how difficult life seemed back then."

"So you left the café and then what happened?"

"Things changed." I shrugged a little, "I changed. My beliefs, actions, approaches.... Some were little things, others were a lot bigger. It wasn't long after I left here I quit what I was doing and decided to go see the world."

"Really?"

I nodded, "I had dreamed about doing that kind of thing for a long time. It always seemed so out there, though. But after coming back from the café, I was more open. I think before when I'd met people who were doing something amazing, I'd put up walls. I'd find a million reasons why I could never do those things, or wasn't doing them. After being here, I saw those same people differently. They weren't a threat anymore. Now they were guides.

"I guess before, I was insecure about who I was. I was so afraid I'd look foolish or feel embarrassed because I didn't know things, that I wouldn't ask. Or worse, wouldn't even put myself in a position to learn.

"Anyway, when I came back from here, I kept crossing paths with interesting people who were out there traveling the world. So after saving up some money, I went out and hit the road too."

Casey nodded, "And?"

I smiled, "More amazing than I could describe in fifty lifetimes. I mean it completely changed my life again. There are *so many* incredible places on this planet. Plus equally amazing experiences to be had. Not to mention life lessons to be learned."

০১ **Chapter 4**

Casey and I talked for almost an hour. I filled her in on the different places I'd been and some of the adventures I'd had. Going on safari in Africa, climbing the great wall of China, exploring the jungles of Borneo, wandering the antiquities of ancient Rome.... I got the impression Casey knew many of the places I spoke of. Something told me she was a traveler too. Yet she was full of questions.

"And what about you?" I finally asked. "I've done almost all the talking. What have you been up to?"

"Well, as you probably noticed, we're not in the same place today as we were last time you visited."

"I was wondering about that."

She nodded, "There's a reason. Something's happening today."

"What is it?"

Just then a white car pulled into the parking lot.

Casey glanced out at it. "Do you know much about cooking, John?"

"Not really. I mean your standard breakfast things I could probably pull off. Why?"

"Mike's going to be coming in a bit late today. I could use some help in the kitchen." She nodded toward the car that had pulled in. "Looks like we have our first customer."

There were lots of reasons why I could have said no. I'd never cooked in a café before. I only knew how to make a few things. I didn't actually work there.... But for some reason, it all seemed perfectly OK.

I smiled, "Well, if they order blueberry pancakes or french toast with pineapple, we're in good shape. Anything other than that, I can't promise much."

She smiled back, "We'll hope for one of those." She glanced out at the car again, "Why don't you head back to the kitchen and look around. I'll check on you in a few minutes."

༺ Chapter 5

Casey watched as a woman got out of the car. She was overdressed by Hawaii standards. Business suit, high heels, hair pinned up.... And overshadowing it all—a very stressed out look. She was also trying to shut the car door, put her keys away, and answer her phone all at the same time.

She succeeded in getting the car door shut, but in the process accidentally dropped the keys to the gravel. Casey heard her say, "shoot" as she bent down to get them. While bending down, she dropped the phone too. Casey smiled.

When the woman had successfully gathered the keys and phone, she walked toward the door to the café. The phone was once again pressed to her ear. As she climbed the steps to enter, she remembered she hadn't locked the door to her car. She fumbled with the keys and dropped them again.

Her irritation showed on her face. Finally, after recovering the keys again, she succeeded in locking the car with a loud beep.

The woman pulled open the door to the café and pressed her phone to her ear as if trying to hear better. "I can't hear you," she said loudly. "The reception is horrible. I can't...I can't...." She looked at the phone. Then, with a sigh of exasperation she turned it off.

"Hi," Casey said in a relaxed voice. She had been standing near the entrance, watching the whole thing.

The woman looked up, surprised. "Hi. Sorry about that. I just...I mean..." The woman shook here head, "I was trying to finish my call, but it seems impossible to get good reception all of a sudden."

Casey nodded, "Yeah, that happens around here." She smiled, "Can I help you?"

The woman looked around. She was evaluating. Stay? Go? Her outfit and demeanor indicated she was looking for somewhere else. Someplace other than a *diner*. Her eyes and facial expression conveyed that the café was beneath her.

But then Casey saw it. An ever so brief flash in the woman's eyes. Under the glossy exterior was an authentic *something* which was saying, "Stay for a while."

"There are lots of other places if you just stay on the road for another twenty minutes or so," Casey said. "You'll get better cell reception there." She was giving the woman an out.

The woman hesitated. So much of her energy wanted to walk out the door. And yet, there was this feeling....

"Or you can stick around for a while," Casey said. "Have a little something and see what you think."

Casey nodded slightly toward a booth by the window, "That's a good seat there."

The woman looked at Casey. Casey looked back.

"OK," the woman said after a few seconds, and then shook her head slightly as if she was trying to clear her mind. "OK, thanks."

She sat down in the booth.

"I'll give you a few minutes to look this over," Casey said and put a menu on the table. "In the meantime, how about something to drink?"

"Coffee. Black."

"Coming right up." Casey turned toward the kitchen. A smile formed on her lips.

Chapter 6

I was still familiarizing myself with the kitchen when Casey came in.

"How's it going?" she asked.

"Well, I found the griddle, the refrigerator, and the utensils."

"And the apron," Casey added.

"And the apron," I said and glanced down. "I hope Mike doesn't mind. I saw it on the back of the door and it called to me."

"I'm sure he won't mind a bit," Casey said.

"What's the story with our customer?"

Casey smiled a very secretive smile, "Too soon to tell. Stay tuned. She pointed behind me. She'd like a cup of black coffee though, can you hand me the coffee pot?"

"I couldn't find the coffee," I replied. "That's what I was looking for when you came in."

Casey pointed behind me and I turned. There was a brand new, fresh pot of coffee sitting on a coffee maker that I *knew* had not been there twenty seconds earlier.

"You sure you need my help?" I asked, and grabbed the coffee pot. I was now remembering that things at the café weren't always what they seemed.

"Absolutely," Casey replied and took the pot from me along with an empty cup from a nearby rack. She smiled, "Hang in there. I'll be back in a minute."

↶ Chapter 7

Casey approached the table. The woman was fiddling with her phone, even though there was no signal. It was habit.

"Here you go. One cup of fresh coffee. Black. Our special Hawaiian blend," Casey said. She put the cup down and filled it. "Still no signal, huh?"

"No," the woman replied, slightly agitated.

Casey put down the coffee pot and extended her hand. "I'm Casey. This is your first time here isn't it?"

The woman cautiously extended her hand and shook Casey's. "Yes, it is. I'm afraid I'm a little lost. I've never been out this way before. I'm Jessica."

"Well, I'm glad you're here, Jessica. Welcome."

Casey reached over and grabbed the menu from the table where she and I had been sitting earlier. "In case you want to stick around for a little while," she said and put the menu next to Jessica.

Jessica glanced at the front of the menu. There was an inscription on the front. Under the lettering which said "Welcome to the Why Are You Here Café" was a small notation. It read, "Prior to ordering, please consult with our wait staff about what your time here could mean."

Jessica pointed at the wording and looked up at Casey, "I don't get it."

Casey smiled, "Over the years we've noticed people seem to feel a little different after they spend some time here. So now we try to ease them into the whole *Why Are You Here Café* experience. Help them understand what they might expect."

Jessica gave Casey a confused look, "I still don't get it."

"Sometimes you go someplace and ask for coffee and you get coffee. Sometimes you ask for coffee and end up getting a lot more than you expect. This is the kind of place where you get a lot more than you expect."

Jessica still looked confused.

"Take a glance and let me know if anything catches your fancy," Casey said and touched the menu. "I'll give you a few minutes."

As Casey turned and started to walk away, Jessica opened the menu.

"This place is strange," she thought to herself. She looked at her cell phone again. Still no signal. "Can't even check to see if there are any customer reviews for it."

"Yeah, we're a little off the beaten path in that regard." It was Casey. She had gathered some items from another table, and was now walking past Jessica on her way to the kitchen. "Gives you a chance to tap into your intuition though. It's more powerful anyway," she said and smiled.

Jessica hesitantly smiled back, unsure of what Casey was talking about. She watched Casey head into the kitchen. "How did she know what I was thinking?" she wondered.

Chapter 8

"How's it going?"

I looked up. I'd been looking in the fridge trying to familiarize myself with all the ingredients inside.

"Good, I guess. Not sure if I'm ready for this."

"You wouldn't be here if you weren't."

"How's our customer?"

"A lot like you were the first time you visited here. She's not sure whether she should stay or go."

I nodded. I remembered what it was like to sit inside the café and try to talk yourself into going. Even though everything inside you said, "*Stay!*"

"Exactly," Casey replied. "She's questioning her intuition, just like you did."

I walked over to a shelf where I'd put my backpack and removed my notebook from the outside pocket. "Funny you should say that. When I first started looking around the kitchen and going through the fridge, part of me was very convinced I would be better off sitting out there." I nodded toward the outside where the booths were.

"But?"

"But one of the biggest lessons I've learned during my travels is to trust my intuition. When you're in places you've never been, interacting in languages you don't understand, and totally testing new waters, you don't have much experience to count on for making decisions. But every time I trusted my intuition, it was always right. I just had to quiet my mind for a minute, and I'd know."

Casey nodded, "Yeah it's kind of nice we're designed with a built in guidance system. Too bad most people turn theirs off."

She glanced at the notebook I was holding, "What's in there?"

"Ideas, thoughts, insights.... My *'aha!'* realizations. I developed a little system after I left here last time. When I discover something significant—have an *'aha!'*

moment—I write it in my notebook. And I do it right away." I laughed, "I've learned the hard way if I don't write things down when they come to me, I forget them."

"What are you writing down this time?"

"Actually, this time I'm circling."

"Circling?"

I nodded, "Like I said, I learned to trust my intuition when I was traveling. I noted that a long time ago. This morning, when I was having doubts about stepping in for Mike, I wasn't trusting my intuition. So I'm circling."

I opened up the notebook, and flipped through it until I found what I was looking for. Then I drew a big circle.

Casey looked at what I'd done. "You circled '*trust my intuition*.'" She laughed, "And from the looks of it, that is not the first time you've circled it."

I laughed too, "No it isn't."

There were about twenty circles all around the words—*trust my intuition*.

"And why do you do that?"

"It's a great way to remind myself. At night, or whenever I've got a few minutes to spare, I flip through my book. The heavily circled items always catch my attention. It's a great way to help me reinforce the big stuff I've learned. Eventually the heavily circled things become habit and I don't find myself re-circling them as much."

"So what happened today?"

I smiled, "Even the best of minds forget now and again?"

She laughed.

"Actually, I think in part it's because I'm back at this place. I'm still so surprised to be here. Coming back reminds me a little bit of who I was when I first came here. I'm so grateful for that night and what it led me to. At the same time, I'm not that guy anymore. So I'm sort of adjusting to this new reality of being back here and also being the person who is me now. Does that possibly make any sense at all?"

Casey looked out the window, "Perfect sense. And it's a good thing you remember how it felt when you first visited here because someone needs to hear that."

"Who?"

"Our customer. She's about to leave because she's afraid to stay."

I looked over the order window and into the café. Sure enough, the woman was starting to gather her things. "I've got this," I said.

"Are you sure?"

I smiled and tapped the open page of my notebook, "Trust my intuition."

∽ Chapter 9

"Hi."

Jessica had gathered her things and was trying to get out of the booth. But she had dropped her keys under the table and was struggling to find them.

She raised her head, "Oh, hi," she replied, clearly flustered.

"Let me help," I said and reached down and grabbed her keys. "Are you heading out?"

She didn't know what to say. I could tell.

"Well, I...I was just..."

"You can go if you want to. It's no problem." I smiled and looked into her eyes, "I have a hunch though that this is where you're supposed to be right now? Is that what you're sensing too?"

She looked at me. She was so confused. I could see it in her eyes. There was so much fear and yet so much of something else too. Hope maybe? She looked away.

I smiled again, "I'm John," I said cheerfully and extended my hand. "I'm the chef here."

"At least for right now," I thought to myself.

"Something tells me if you stick around and let me make you one of my special breakfasts, you're going to have a whole new perspective about life in an hour or so."

I said it flippantly. Like it was just a fun invitation to a *really really* good breakfast. I didn't want to freak her out with the fact that she probably *would* have an entirely new perspective by the time she left.

She hesitated. She was still planning on leaving, I could sense it.

I lowered my voice and leaned toward her a little. Then I asked in my most cute and charming manner, "Can you keep a secret?"

In spite of herself, she smiled, "Sure."

"Today is my first day on the job. And you are my very first customer. If you leave, I really think they might lose confidence in me." I smiled and pretended to be worried, "I may even lose a little confidence in myself."

She smiled again. It was working.

"You wouldn't want that on your conscious would you? I know I can be great at this. And if you stay, I have a hunch it will be my big break."

She looked at me. I smiled. She hesitated. Then she put her things back on the table.

"Thanks," I said. "You won't regret it. I promise."

She sat down and picked up her phone. Habit again.

"Not really much signal here," I commented. "Great conversations though, trust me." I nodded toward the menu on the table. "I'll give you a minute to glance at that, and then Casey will come back to take your order. OK?"

She nodded.

I turned and started to head back to the kitchen.

"Jessica," she said.

I turned around, "Excuse me?"

She smiled. It was a good smile, a genuine smile. The kind of smile you can't fake. She hadn't decided to stick around because of my little story. She was trusting her intuition, and now her whole being was telling her it was the right decision.

"My name is Jessica," she said again.

I smiled back, "Nice to meet you, Jessica. Thanks for sticking around. You'll be glad you did."

Chapter 10

"Your turn," I said as I came through the swinging door into the kitchen.

Casey laughed, "Someone was putting on the charm out there."

"So far so good. If she orders anything other than french toast with pineapple, or blueberry pancakes though, the charm is going to be long on promise and short on delivery."

Casey smiled and exited through the doors.

"So, have you decided," she said when she approached Jessica's table.

Jessica nodded, "I'm going to stick around for a little while. I just talked with your chef."

"How'd that go."

Jessica smiled, "He's funny."

"What did he say to convince you?"

"You know, I think I was trying to convince myself to go. I don't really know what I'm doing here and I have all these obligations to take care of today.... But somehow his conversation reminded me of some promises I keep making to myself and then keep breaking."

"Which are?"

"To relax more. Enjoy life. And when I'm not sure, trust my intuition."

Casey smiled, "He circled it for you."

"What?" Jessica replied and looked confused.

"I'll explain later. Or he will."

Casey nodded toward the menu, "Have you decided?"

* * *

A few minutes later, Casey approached the order window. She took off the piece of paper where she'd written Jessica's order and attached it to the circular spinner. She looked at me through the window and smiled, "Order in."

As she walked away, I made my way to the counter and spun the wheel so I could see the order ticket. "Got to love this place," I said and smiled.

I put the ticket on the cutting table next to the stove. "One order of pineapple french toast coming right up," I said to myself.

᥈᥈ Chapter 11

Jessica had watched as Casey brought her order to the kitchen. "I still think this place is a little strange," she thought to herself.

She picked up her phone again, but then remembered there was no signal.

As she put the phone down, she noticed a tiny little piece of wording on the bottom of the menu. The front of the menu was facing up. There was the name of the café, the words about asking your wait staff, and then at the very bottom was an arrow. Next to that it said—*turn me over*.

She flipped the menu over. It was blank except for three questions.

Why are you here?
Are you playing in your playground?
Do you have MPO?

"OK, now it has gone from strange to very strange," she thought to herself. She read the questions again.

"I have no idea why I'm here, I haven't played in a playground since I was a kid, and what the heck is MPO?"

She turned the menu back over and picked up her phone. No signal. She knew that. Why did she keep picking up her phone?

"Sometimes habits take a while to break."

It was Casey.

"Can I give you a refill on the coffee?"

Jessica nodded, "Sure." She looked at her phone. "I think I'm addicted to that thing. I feel like I've picked it up a dozen times since I've been here. I must do that constantly and not even realize it."

Jessica looked around, "Is it always this empty?"

Casey shook her head, "Only when it needs to be."

Jessica didn't understand. She started to reach for her phone again, then remembered. She didn't want to appear stupid, so she pretended she was reaching for the menu and flipped it over. There were the three questions again.

"I see you've discovered those," Casey said.

"A few minutes ago," Jessica replied.

"And?"

Jessica didn't know what to say.

"Uh...interesting..."

She hoped that would end the conversation. She felt very self-conscious all of a sudden. Like she didn't belong there. For a brief moment she thought of making up some excuse and leaving.

Casey smiled, "It's OK. Most people aren't quite sure what to think the first time they see them."

The panicky feeling started to subside. Casey seemed so calm. So with it. It was disconcerting and comforting at the same time.

"What do they mean?" Jessica asked.

"Well, like I mentioned earlier, sometimes you go someplace for coffee and you get coffee. Sometimes you get a lot more. Based on those questions, I'd say you're here for a lot more."

Jessica looked at her. Calming presence or not, this waitress was very confusing. "Doesn't everyone get the same menu?" she asked.

"Uh huh," Casey replied and smiled. "Just not the same questions."

Just then the order up bell rang. Casey and Jessica both looked toward the kitchen.

"That was fast," Casey said. "Let me see what John's got for you."

She left the table and headed toward the kitchen.

Jessica breathed a little sigh. The conversation had been strange. She felt strange. Like she was in the middle of a play and didn't know what the next line was supposed to be. She looked down at the menu again.

Why are you here?
Are you playing in your playground?
Do you have MPO?

෨ **Chapter 12**

Casey walked up to the order window. There was a tray on top of it and on the tray was a fruit bowl. Fresh papaya, lime wedges, shredded fresh coconut, and mint leaves on top.

"Interesting looking french toast," she said and smiled at me.

"A little breakfast appetizer. Courtesy of the chef," I replied.

"How do you know she likes papaya?"

I smiled, "Intuition. There were a dozen things in the fridge I considered, but something said go with the papaya."

"OK."

Casey grabbed the tray and brought it to Jessica's table.

"And here is your french toast," she said and put the plate in front of Jessica.

Jessica looked at the papaya. She didn't know what to say.

"Just kidding," Casey added and smiled. "This is a little pre-breakfast, breakfast, for you. Courtesy of John."

Jessica looked toward the kitchen. I saw her looking my way, and waved. She waved back, looking a little self-conscious. It made me laugh. During my first visit to the café, I'd been the one feeling self-conscious about waving to someone in the kitchen.

"Tell me if it's good," Casey said. "I'm starving and I'm going to ask him to make one for me if you like it."

Jessica squeezed the lime onto the papaya and speared a piece with her fork, along with some of the mint leaf. Her face lit up as she chewed the combination. "It's good," she said, when she'd finished the bite. "Really good."

She glanced at the plate and before she could convince herself not to, she said, "I will never eat all this *and* french toast too." She looked around the café, "I know this sounds strange, but unless you have someone else to take care of, why don't you share it with me."

Casey smiled, "Are you sure?"

Jessica wasn't sure. But she nodded yes anyway.

Casey grabbed a plate and fork from the counter behind her and slid in across the booth from Jessica. Jessica noticed that the plate and fork had been sitting right there. Almost as if Casey somehow knew she was going to be invited.

"Impossible," Jessica thought to herself.

"What's that?" Casey asked and smiled.

For a brief moment, Jessica didn't know if she had said *"impossible"* out loud or not. She was sure she hadn't. But...

"Wow, you're right. This *is* good," Casey said.

Jessica re-directed her focus back to Casey, who had just taken a bite of the fruit.

"Isn't it?" she replied.

They each took another bite, then Casey tapped on the menu, "You seemed pretty drawn to these questions when I came to the table a few minutes ago."

"It's not exactly the kind of thing you normally find on a menu," Jessica replied. "I'm not even sure I know what they mean."

Casey nodded, "Yeah they aren't the type of questions you get asked very often." She took another small bite of fruit. "They're big ones though."

Jessica looked at the questions. She had the sudden urge to open up her heart and tell this waitress everything. Her sadness, her frustrations, the way she felt like she was living someone else's life.... No, that would be ridiculous. She didn't even know this woman. Besides, people don't care. You just keep it to yourself and keep pushing forward.

But the feeling wouldn't go away. It was an aching that seemed to come from nowhere and then spread through her entire body.

"What am I doing here?" she asked softly.

Casey looked up from the fruit. Her eyes focused on Jessica's, "That's a good question. A good place to start," she replied gently.

Jessica looked around the café, "Where am I? What is this place?"

Casey smiled, "You're in an unusual place full of unusual opportunities."

Jessica looked at her confused, "I don't know what that means. It sounds mysterious."

"It is."

Jessica felt it again. The urge to pour out her heart. It was an aching, a need from somewhere deep in her soul. Then without knowing why, she started to cry. She looked down at the table. After a few minutes of silence, she looked up at Casey.

"I'm lost," she said in a quiet voice, as the tears rolled down her cheeks. "I'm really lost."

Casey nodded, "I know."

Jessica reached up and brushed the tears from her face. They were replaced with new tears. "What do you mean you know?"

"This is the place where lost people go to be found."

๑๑ Chapter 13

I looked out at the table where Casey and Jessica were sitting. It looked like Jessica was crying. She looked confused, and unsure.

"Welcome to The Why Café," I thought.

It looked like Jessica might leave. She had that sense about her. That it might be more than she could take.

"Stay for a while," I said under my breath. "It will get better. I promise it will."

I could hear food simmering behind me. Time to flip the french toast.

I turned back to the stove and adjusted the items on the griddle. Memories from my first experience at the café came flashing back. I remembered that I too had considered leaving. But I didn't. Yes the place had seemed a little strange. Yes the menu questions had thrown me. Something had seemed very right though. So I'd stayed. It was a good choice. A life changing choice. Somehow I knew if Jessica stayed, it would be the same for her.

I glanced back out at the table and saw Casey looking my way. She nodded and smiled. It was like she knew what I was thinking. I smiled back and then turned to the stove again, "Welcome to The Why Café," I said to myself.

* * *

Jessica was wiping her tears with her napkin. She had stopped crying.

Casey looked at her, "Tears are powerful signs. It means something matters to you. Sometimes it's the only way our heart knows how to communicate to the rest of our being that it knows something."

Jessica nodded. She wasn't sure what Casey meant, but something about it sounded right.

"I think your heart is telling you to stick around for a while."

Jessica nodded again, "I think so too," she said quietly.

The menu was still sitting on the table. The three questions were facing upward.

Casey tapped her finger next to the first one. Jessica looked down.

Why are you here?

"What is your heart saying right now?" Casey asked gently.

Jessica looked up, "My heart feels empty. And it's tired of feeling empty. It's telling me there's supposed to be more to life than a heart that feels empty."

Casey smiled, "That sounds like a great piece of wisdom." She paused a moment, "A few seconds ago you asked almost the identical question that's on the menu. You asked—*What am I doing here?* What did you mean by that?"

Jessica shook her head, "I don't know really. It just came out." She hesitated, "Isn't there supposed to be more to life? Isn't it supposed to be fun, or interesting, or exciting...? I've been pushing and pushing in so many aspects of my life. Now I'm sitting here crying at a café in the middle of nowhere, talking with a complete stranger. And the overriding feeling I get is that somehow I've missed something."

She looked away, "Because I'm not having fun, and it doesn't seem interesting, and I'm not all that excited about life."

Casey smiled, "Do you like the ocean?"

Jessica looked back at her, "I used to. That was one of the whole reasons why I came to Hawaii. I wanted to be surrounded by the ocean...to experience it every day."

"And?"

"I don't even notice it anymore."

Casey smiled again, "Follow me." She got up from the table and grabbed a tray from the counter. She put their plates, silverware, glasses, and the bowl of fruit on the tray. "Come on," she said, and nodded with her head toward a door at the far end of the café.

૭૦ Chapter 14

The view took Jessica's breath away. She worked in a very expensive office building overlooking a prime piece of Hawaii coastline. It was very pretty. Nothing like this though. This was perfection. It was the essence of what postcards tried to convey and adventure seekers dreamed of.

A moment before, she and Casey had exited the café through a very innocuous looking door at the far end of the building. "Every door goes somewhere," Casey had said. "You only know where when you walk through it."

This one had certainly gone somewhere.

As they'd exited through the door, they stepped onto the most beautiful beach Jessica had ever seen. The water was a majestic turquoise blue. And as she watched the waves form and crest before they crashed down, the foamy white tops and interior of the waves took on an iridescent shine.

The sand was amazing. A glistening whitish yellow.

Jessica reached down and grabbed a handful. It was so pure. Tiny grains, soft to the touch. She let it fall through her fingers.

She looked up. It was what she had envisioned when she decided to come to Hawaii. Giant coconut palms swayed in the breeze. She could smell the ocean.

"Where are we?" she asked, surprised.

"Paradise," Casey replied. "Also behind The Why Café. This is our special ocean view seating area."

Jessica turned and looked back at the café. There was just the back wall of the building, the door they'd just walked through, and then sand.

She turned back to the ocean and gave Casey a confused look, "I don't understand."

Casey nodded toward the café.

Jessica turned and looked again.

This time there were bamboo tables and bamboo chairs sitting under a thatched roof area which extended from the café.

"How did...?" Jessica began.

"Almost forgot," Casey said and smiled. "We need to tell John we're out here."

She walked to the wall which was the back of the café. Then reached for a latch that Jessica was sure hadn't been there moments before. In a second, a portion of the top half of the wall came down and folded under. It created an order counter, similar to the one on the inside. Only instead of looking out from the kitchen into the café, this one looked out from the kitchen onto the magnificent ocean view.

"Did I miss something?" I asked a little surprised as the back of the kitchen wall folded down.

"Not anymore," Casey replied and smiled.

I looked out at the beach and ocean. "Wow! That's some view."

"I thought you'd like it. How about if we serve Jessica out here instead of inside the café? I think a little of this outdoor energy will do her good."

"Fine by me. Her order is almost ready." I looked out at the view again. It was truly spectacular. The ocean, the palm trees, the sand.... In the distance I could just make out two people bobbing in the waves. They were sitting on surfboards.

For a brief moment as I was watching them, I could have sworn one of the surfers *waved* at me. I shielded my eyes a bit and looked again, but both surfers were now racing down the front of a wave.

"Couldn't have been," I thought.

ꙮ Chapter 15

Casey picked up the order of pineapple french toast from the counter where I'd placed it. She brought it over to the table Jessica was sitting at. There really wasn't a bad table in the back beach area. Jessica had selected one that didn't have the best view though.

"If you'd like, you're welcome to take one of those," Casey said and nodded toward the two tables with the best views.

Jessica glanced at the tables. She hesitated. "No, it's OK," she replied after a moment. "This is fine."

Casey smiled, "Are you sure?"

Jessica hesitated again. She looked at the tables a second time. "No, really, this is fine. I'm fine."

Casey nodded, "It's OK to want more than fine."

Jessica hesitated once more as an internal dialogue played out in her head.

Casey stood and waited patiently. After a few seconds she said, "Maybe try one of those out for a minute or two and see if you like it better. If not, you can always come back here."

It was the nudge Jessica was waiting for. She got up and walked the short distance to one of the tables with the best view of the beach. Casey followed, still carrying her food.

Jessica sat down.

"Well?" Casey asked.

Jessica smiled. It was the first totally open smile Casey had seen from her since she arrived.

"This *is* better," she said. "Thanks."

Casey put the tray of food on the table. As she did, Jessica commented, "I don't know why I do that."

"What do you mean?"

"I accept fine. I saw this table. I really wanted to come over here. I just..." Jessica paused.

"Sometimes it isn't that important," Casey interjected. "What we have really is OK with us. Sometimes though, we get ourselves into a pattern where we're willing to accept less than what we really want. The people who have dined here at the café have figured out if you keep doing that, you don't end up very happy."

"You just end up fine," Jessica added.

Casey smiled, "Exactly."

One by one, Casey picked up the items on the tray and set them on the table. "Here you go," she said. "Pineapple french toast, our specialty of the house. Also, some homemade coconut syrup if you're willing to try something a little different."

Jessica nodded.

"And lastly, some fresh pineapple juice."

Covering the top of the glass of juice was a little umbrella made from paper and wood. Jessica picked it up and smiled. A chunk of pineapple was speared onto its handle. Jessica ate the pineapple and then opened and closed the little umbrella a few times.

"I used to love these when I was a little girl," she said thoughtfully. "My mother had five of them, and every morning at breakfast, she would put one in my juice." Jessica sighed, "She must have washed them hundreds of times, but somehow they held together.

"I don't even know where she got them. Our area was so poor.... My brothers couldn't have cared less, but I loved them. It was something so small, but somehow..." she paused. "Somehow it gave me something to look forward to every day."

She opened and closed the umbrella again then set it on the table far away from her. "That was a long time ago," she said, the emotion gone from her voice. Her smile was gone too.

Casey nodded, "It's nice to have something to look forward to every day. I see why it meant a lot to you."

Casey moved the tray to one of the other tables and sat across from Jessica. "Can I ask you something?"

Jessica looked up, "Sure."

"Do you like helping people?"

"What do you mean?"

"Do you like helping people? Doing things for others? Helping them?"

Jessica nodded, "Yes."

"Do you have an easier time helping others than letting them help you?"

Jessica tipped her head to the side a little and smiled, "Yes."

Casey nodded and paused, "Why are you being so selfish?"

Immediately Jessica's posture changed. She sat back in her chair, distancing herself from Casey.

"What do you mean by that? I'm not selfish," she replied with an edge in her voice.

Casey looked at her, with a soft smile on her face, "Why do you like helping people?"

Jessica hesitated. The edge was still there in her voice. "Because they *like* to get help? It, it..." she stammered. "It *helps* them!"

"I'm sure it does."

Jessica looked away, then back at Casey. Her voice softened a bit, "It makes me feel good."

Casey gave her an inquisitive look.

"It makes me feel good," Jessica said again. "When I help people it makes me feel good. That's why I like doing it."

Casey nodded, "I think that's the same for most people who like to help others."

Casey said nothing else.

Jessica looked out at the ocean. Her face softened, "I am being selfish, aren't I? I'm keeping from everyone else the exact thing I love to receive—the chance to feel good."

She turned and looked at Casey, "My whole life I've been that way. I never want to impose on others. I never want to inconvenience them.... So I always run away when people offer to help." She looked down, "I never realized what I was keeping from them."

Casey nodded, knowingly. "It's often those who give the most who have the hardest time receiving," she said and smiled. "Until they come to the same realization you just came to."

Jessica looked at Casey, "Why did you share that with me?"

Casey smiled, "I have a hunch it will come in handy before the day is over."

೦೦ **Chapter 16**

A warm breeze was coming through the opening and into the kitchen. I took a long breath of the ocean air and looked out at the waves. "Wow, I love Hawaii," I thought to myself.

Casey and Jessica were sitting at a table and talking. No one else had come into the café, so I was standing in the kitchen having a few pieces of french toast.

I looked out at the ocean again. "The surfers are gone," I said to myself. I scanned the waves but couldn't see them. The waves looked perfect and I wondered if I could rent a board out this way.

"You can borrow mine," a voice said.

I looked out the window and in the direction of the sound. Although I already knew who was there.

"Mike!" I said and smiled. The fact that he had read my mind was already lost to me. I was so happy to see him. The last time had been when I'd first visited the café.

Standing next to him was a little girl. "Are you John?" she asked.

I leaned out onto the counter and looked out at her. "Yes I am," I replied and smiled. "How did you know that?"

"My Dad told me you'd be here today."

"*I* didn't even know I'd be here today," I thought to myself. "How did he...?"

"I'm Emma," the little girl said.

I returned my attention to her, "Nice to meet you, Emma."

She grabbed Mike's arm, "Can I go say hi to Casey?"

Mike nodded and she ran off toward where Casey and Jessica were sitting. He watched her run to the table and then turned back to me. He was smiling. "Good to see you again, John," he said and extended his hand across the counter.

I shook it, "Good to be back. I nodded in the direction of the ocean. You've moved."

"Something like that," he said and smiled again. "We got inspired by this one customer who talked about franchising. The next thing you know...."

Like Casey had earlier, he was referencing a comment I'd made the first time I'd been at the café.

I laughed, "I wonder who that guy was?"

"A good guy," Mike replied. "A very good guy who was about to start on a really big adventure."

A burst of laughter erupted from the table where Casey and Jessica were sitting. Mike and I both looked over and saw Emma doing something silly. It looked like she was imitating an ocean animal, and she was making her eyes as big as possible while she danced around.

"Looks like I'm not the only one who's been on a big adventure since last time I was here," I said.

Mike turned back to me, "It's the best thing I've ever done. It's definitely not for everyone, I won't kid you. For me though, it's been amazing."

"How old is she?"

"She just turned seven."

"She seems pretty self-confident for seven. Although considering who she hangs out with, that doesn't surprise me."

"She's an amazing little girl. She really is."

"Was that the two of you I saw surfing earlier?"

"That was us. And after a full morning of surfing, we are more than ready for a big breakfast. So what's on the menu today?"

I smiled, "Last time I was here you were the chef in this place. Is that no longer the case?"

He smiled back, "Well, as long as you're OK with it, you get the call today. Time to take things to the next level."

I really wasn't sure what to say. I didn't know much about cooking, that was for sure. It felt right though. Something about the whole scene felt right.

"OK," I replied. "As long as I can tap you for a little guidance as needed."

"You've got a deal."

I reached back and grabbed a couple of menus which were sitting on a counter behind me. "I'm sure you know exactly what's on here, but feel free to take a look and let me know what I can get for you."

He took the menus and turned them over. "And about these?" he asked and pointed to the three questions.

"The basis for life-changing conversation," I replied and smiled.

◎ Chapter 17

Casey and Jessica watched as Emma ran back to Mike. Emma had been recounting the events of the morning to them. How they'd seen a spotted ray leap out of the water while they were surfing. And they had surfed right past a dolphin when they dropped into one of their waves.

"She's so full of life," Jessica said.

"Uh huh," Casey replied and smiled.

"Is she always like that?"

"Pretty much. Mike's done an amazing job of letting her play in her playground."

"Is Mike her Dad?"

"Yes, that's him over there." Casey motioned toward where Mike was.

"Do they eat here a lot?"

Casey laughed, "Pretty often. He owns the place."

"Oh."

Jessica watched them for a moment, then turned back to Casey. "Sorry," she said and shook her head. "I heard your answer a moment ago but got distracted. What did you say when I asked if Emma is always so full of energy?"

Casey smiled, "I said Mike does an amazing job of letting her play in her playground." Then Casey glanced down at the menu which was still sitting on the table.

Jessica followed her gaze. The back of the menu was facing up. There were the three questions she had seen earlier.

Why are you here?
Are you playing in your playground?
Do you have MPO?

Jessica looked at the menu then looked up at Casey. "OK," she said. "You've got my curiosity. What's the deal with the playground?"

"Did you play when you were a kid?" Casey asked her.

"Well, that was a long time ago. I'd have to give that some thought. I mean…"

Casey leaned forward and looked at Jessica. Her movement caused Jessica to pause. "You know," Casey said, "how we were talking before about people who have an easier time helping others than accepting help? One of the ways that shows itself is they hesitate to talk about themselves."

Casey let that sink in. "I'm asking because I genuinely want to know."

"Got it."

Casey smiled, "Did you play when you were a kid?"

Jessica shook her head, "Not a lot." She paused, "I had kind of a tough childhood."

Casey waited, but Jessica didn't explain further. "Do you remember anything you did which you liked?"

Jessica looked away. She seemed to be sifting through lots of old memories. "When I was little I used to play on the swings," she finally said, and then turned back toward Casey. "There was a park at the end of my street. When things would get really rough at home, I'd run to the park and swing on the swings. Sometimes for hours. That was where they always found me."

Casey nodded, "Why that?"

"I don't know. I guess it was my refuge. There were two swings attached to a giant tree. There was almost no one who used the park, so I almost always had the swings to myself. The tree was huge and would cover me in shade. I'd swing as high as I could until I felt the emptiness beneath me. You know that moment when you're at the top of the swinging motion?"

Jessica paused, "I used to wish I could hold onto that moment and just float. I'd pretend I was a little cloud and I was being born. And if I could only learn to float freely for a few seconds more, I could escape up into the sky. Then I could leave all the rest of it behind. Forever."

A tear started to form at the corner of Jessica's eye. She quickly brushed it away. "But you can't. No matter how hard you try, no matter how high I would swing, I always came back down. I always had to go back there."

"But not anymore."

"No, not anymore. I left when I was seventeen and I've never gone back."

"And you've been pushing hard ever since."

Jessica looked out to the ocean, "Ever since."

೬೨ **Chapter 18**

"Hi, Coconut."

Mike picked Emma up and put her on a stool next to the serving window and counter.

"That's my Dad's nickname for me," Emma explained to me. "He says it's because when I was little I used to be the size of a coconut."

I smiled.

"Did you say hi to Casey?" Mike asked her.

"Uh huh. And to Jessica too. That's her friend who's with her. I told them about the ray and the dolphin we saw this morning."

"Oh, cool. Well, John is our guest chef for the day. How about some breakfast?"

"OK."

"What would you like?"

I was hoping she'd say french toast with pineapple.

"Hmm. How about an omelete and pancakes with fruit."

Mike nodded, "Sounds good. Why don't you tell the chef."

Emma turned on her stool and looked at me, "Can I help you make it?"

I looked at Mike.

"Fine with me," he said, "as long as you're OK with it."

I turned to Emma, "Sounds perfect. Why don't you come in and we'll make everything together."

Emma jumped off her stool and headed for the door.

"Anything for you, Mike?" I asked.

He smiled, "How about french toast with pineapple. And if you don't mind, while you and Emma are cooking, I'm going to wash off the surfboards."

"No problem. We'll call you when everything's ready."

I turned back to the kitchen and started getting some items together. A moment later the door opened and Emma came through. I noticed right away the way she walked. It was with a lightness and an energy I didn't often see with adults. Sort of like walking, dancing and skipping all at the same time. As if she couldn't wait to get to wherever she was going.

"Where should we start?" I asked.

"I'll get the ingredients," she replied. "I don't like the cutting part, so can you do that?"

"Sure. How about I cut and you stir?"

"OK."

We put all the ingredients on the counter, and began preparing things to make the omelet, pancakes, and Mike's french toast.

"My dad says you're on an adventure. Is that true?" Emma asked.

I nodded, "Sort of."

"What kind of an adventure?"

"Well, the last time I saw your dad, I was kind of confused about what I wanted to do with my life."

"Were you sad?"

"No, not sad really. More like I felt like my life was passing by and I wasn't doing as many fun and interesting things as I wanted to be doing."

"So you went on an adventure?"

"Well, I started off by thinking about what type of adventure I wanted to go on. Then once I knew, I saved up some money for a couple of years, and then I went."

"Where did you go?"

"I went around the world."

Emma looked at me with a surprised look. "You saw the *whole* world?"

I smiled, "Well, I traveled around the world. I didn't see it all, not on that one trip. I visited a lot of places though."

"Did you go on other trips?"

I smiled again. She had such wonderful energy to her. "I did. As a matter of fact, I'm just coming back from a trip now. I was traveling in Africa, Central America, and South East Asia."

"Do you work?"

I laughed, "Sometimes. After my first trip I decided I liked traveling so much, that I wanted to do a lot more of it. So ever since then I work for a year, then travel for a year. Work for another year, travel for another year."

"You must be a good saver. My dad gives me an allowance every week. Sometimes I save it for something I really want. Other times I just spend it right away."

"Well, I think you've already learned a great life lesson then."

"What's that?"

"When you know what you want, it makes it a lot easier to save for it."

"That's true. There was this one surfboard I really really wanted. My dad made me a deal. He said if I saved up enough for half of it, he would pay for the other half."

"And did you get it?"

She nodded enthusiastically, "That's the blue one I was carrying when we walked up."

"Was it hard to save for it?"

"Sometimes. I mean, there were other things I wanted to buy too, like these little plastic ponies, which I really like, and some other toys.... But I kept comparing them to having my surfboard and I wanted my surfboard more. Plus, one day my friend's sister let me borrow her surfboard, which is the same kind as the one I wanted.... After that it was a lot easier to save. Because trust me, once you've tried *that* surfboard, you know you want that the most."

I smiled. She was so animated when she talked, and so unabashedly honest. "That's pretty much the same for me and travel," I said. "When I was trying to sort things out, I went on a trip to Costa Rica..."

"My dad loves Costa Rica!" Emma interjected.

I smiled again, "I remember that. Well, Costa Rica was one of the first places I traveled outside of my own country. And I had such a great time that when I came home, it was a lot easier for me to save my money for my next trip."

"Kind of like with me and my surfboard."

I nodded, "Uh huh. Pretty much the same."

I poured the ingredients I'd been chopping into a bowl and handed it to Emma. "OK, you are our stirring specialist. Ready to stir?"

"Ready to stir!" She grabbed a spoon and began stirring super fast. Items started sloshing out of the bowl.

I laughed, "Maybe we should keep it *in* the bowl?"

She laughed too and slowed down her stirring. Then she held up her spoon. "Ready to cook!" she said.

⌒ Chapter 19

Casey took a long look at Jessica, "Thank you for telling me about the swings." She paused, "Maybe it's time to re-visit your playground."

Jessica shook her head, "No, I'm not going back there. Not ever. That's done with."

Casey nodded, "I don't mean go back to that place, or those people. Maybe it's time to re-visit your personal playground."

Jessica looked across the table at Casey, "What do you mean?"

"Earlier you mentioned Emma's energy. How she seems so full of life. All of us have that within us. It's just sometimes we've forgotten. We've closed our playground."

Casey could see Jessica was confused.

"Think of it like this," Casey began. "Kids have this innate sense of what they like and don't like. Maybe they like going on the slide, but they don't like the climbing area. Or they like the swings but not the monkey bars.... They just know. And in their world, it makes perfect sense that if you like it, you do it. If you don't like it, you don't do it."

"If only they knew the truth and how that changes," Jessica said.

"Well that's the thing," Casey continued. "Maybe they *do* know the truth. Only it's the rest of us who change."

Jessica looked up. Something had struck a chord. She put her arms to her side and shook them a little.

"What is it?" Casey asked.

"Oh, nothing. Sorry. It's just that..."

"What?"

"Well, when you said that, about maybe they do know the truth but it's the rest of us who change...I got chills all of a sudden. It's nothing...really."

"Or maybe it's everything," Casey said softly. "Maybe that's *you* speaking to *you*. Saying, 'Hey, we just realized something very important.'"

Jessica didn't reply.

"When we're kids, we know what we like," Casey continued. "We know what parts of the playground excite us. We do our best to fill as much time as we can every day with those."

"And then what happens?"

"That depends on the child. Some keep their playground open. They may change the rides as they get older. But they never lose touch with the idea that they can spend their life playing."

"And others?"

"The vast majority of people fall into the 'others' category."

"What happens to them?"

"Well, again, everyone's story is different. In some cases they allow others to tell them they can't play anymore. Or they need to grow up. Their world becomes one of 'have to', 'need to', 'can't', 'shouldn't', 'must', and a host of other words which confine them. Sometimes they even adopt those words on their own."

"And what happens to their playground?"

"Over time it gets less and less use. The weeds grow. The grass gets tall. The rides start to disappear from sight. In some cases, people build walls around their playground."

"Walls?"

"Sure. I'm too old. I'm not good enough. I'm not smart enough. I don't have enough time.... Those are all walls which keep them from their playground. And there are dozens more just like those.

"As time passes, even the walls start to become overgrown. Plants grow over them, vines crawl up them. They get so covered, people don't even remember the walls are there, let alone that there's a playground beyond the walls."

Casey looked at Jessica, "And sometimes people put a lock on their playground."

Jessica looked away.

"Sometimes they want to run as far as they can from their past. The pain of remembering they had a playground, and they had dreams...is very bad. So not only do they build walls around their playground, but one day they go up to the gate and they put a big lock on it. 'No more,' they say. 'Never again will I believe. Never again will I allow myself to play.'"

"What happens to those people?" Jessica asked in a whisper. She was holding back tears.

"In some cases, they become bitter. The anger, the disappointment, the strain of wanting to believe but not allowing themselves to believe, eats at them. It becomes a toxin they endure every day. They shut out the world because they don't want to be hurt anymore. But they just end up hurting themselves."

Jessica began sobbing. Her shoulders heaved.

"I don't know what to do anymore," she said.

All pretenses were gone now. The clothes, the look, the car.... The outward trappings covering the inner pain were no longer relevant.

"I put the lock on my playground a long time ago. And I swore I would never allow myself to be hurt again. But I'm tired of keeping those walls up. I'm tired of running away all the time. I just want to be..." she hesitated.

"Free?" Casey asked gently.

Jessica nodded, "Free," she whispered. "Only I don't know how to get free."

Casey looked at her, "Most people try to cover the pain with short term attempts to gain their freedom. They drink. They use substances. They shop for things they don't care about. They create excessive drama in their lives.... They want to feel alive and free and so they do all those things. Only those just end up leading to more pain."

"I know that," Jessica replied quietly. "I've been living that. I'm *still* living it."

"Then maybe you'll be one of the ones who chooses the other path."

"Which path is that?"

"For some people, they get tired of holding up the walls. They get tired of not being able to see their playground. And they get tired of the fatigue which comes from short term attempts at freedom which just end up building more walls.

"So one day they decide to make one of the biggest leaps of faith there is. They decide to go rebuild their playground again."

"Is that possible?"

Casey nodded, "Yes. It's always possible. No matter how old someone is, or what their life situation has become. It's always possible."

Jessica sat silently for a few moments. Then she looked at Casey, "How would I start?"

"Slowly. Gently. Or like a giant bulldozer which breaks through everything in it's path…. Everyone is different. That's your choice. What isn't different is that one day you'll decide to cut the lock off your playground. That's the first step. To allow yourself back in.

"Then piece by piece, you'll take the vines away from the walls. And you'll see those walls for what they really are. Not protective barriers to keep you safe, but false realities you constructed which have imprisoned you ever since. Often, in that instant, when you allow yourself to really see them for what they are, the walls just disappear."

"That seems hard to imagine," Jessica said.

"I know," Casey replied. "Yet it's true. And once those walls are gone, you'll see connections to what used to be in your playground. Those will inspire you to cut away the high grass and the underbrush.

"You'll start to be able to see what used to make you happy. You may not still want all of it in your playground. Or maybe you'll still want it, but in different ways. And then you'll start to re-build. A new place, a new playground."

"A new life," Jessica said.

Casey nodded.

"But how can you be so sure it's possible?" Jessica asked.

Casey stood up from the table and gathered a few of the plates. She looked at Jessica, "Because I have been through all of those phases. There was a day in my life when I got tired of hiding, and running, and pretending.... And that was the day I cut the lock off my own playground, and began to rebuild."

Chapter 20

I glanced out the window. Casey had just gotten up from the table where she and Jessica had been sitting. I'd noticed earlier that they were having some pretty intense discussions.

"Welcome to The Why Café," I thought to myself again.

"Pancakes are ready to flip," Emma said.

"Right, I'm on it."

I grabbed a spatula and flipped the pancakes. "Almost ready. Should be just another minute on this side, and then it's time to eat for you and your dad."

"What about my omelet?"

To be honest, I'd been hoping Emma would forget about the omelet. I looked at her, "Emma, I'm sorry, but I don't know how to make an omelet."

"But we cut up all the ingredients already."

I nodded, "Yeah, I know. That part I knew how to do. But not the actual omelet part."

"That's OK."

I breathed a little internal sigh of relief. I was glad she wasn't disappointed.

"You just need a 'Who'," she said.

"A what?"

She giggled, "No. A *Who*!"

I flipped the pancakes onto a plate and Emma put on the fruit I'd cut earlier.

"Whenever you don't know how to do something, you just find someone who knows how to do it. Then you ask them for help. Then they show you, and then you know too. It's *super* easy. That's how I learned almost everything I know how to do."

I smiled. Leave it to a seven year old to break down one of the biggest barriers for most people into something so simple it could be explained in seconds.

"Who taught you that?" I asked.

"My dad."

"Is he a good Who?"

She nodded emphatically, "Uh huh. He knows a lot of stuff. He's the one who taught me to surf."

"Really. What's the most important thing you've learned about surfing?"

She struck a little pose, with her hand on her hip, "You're never going to learn to surf if you never get in the water."

I laughed, "I'm sure that's true."

Just then Mike walked in, "How's breakfast coming?"

"John needs a Who, Dad. Can you show him how to make an omelet?"

I smiled, "Emma has been teaching me about finding a 'Who' when I don't know 'how'."

"Oh, she's great at that."

Mike grabbed a skillet, "OK, super easy…"

As Mike was walking me through the finer points of cooking an omelet, Casey walked in.

She patted Mike on the shoulder. "Smells good in here," she said.

"We made pancakes and french toast, and Dad is teaching John how to make my omelet," Emma replied.

Casey put the plates she was carrying into the sink.

"How's Jessica?" I asked.

"I think she could use a few minutes with you," Casey replied.

I looked over my shoulder at her, "Really? It seemed like you two were in some pretty intense conversations."

"We were. Now I think she could use a few minutes with you. I think she needs to hear your story."

"Go ahead," Mike said. "I'll finish this up. It's almost done anyway."

"OK," I replied a little hesitantly. I wasn't really sure about this. Earlier I'd just gone with my intuition and went right out and talked with her. I wasn't getting any sudden flashes of insight at the moment though.

"You will when you get there," Casey said and threw me a towel.

I wiped my hands and threw it back to her.

"Emma, can we finish our surf conversation a little later?" I asked. "I'd love to hear the other things you've learned about surfing."

She looked up at me and then held a small bowl of syrup over her pancakes. "Syrup volcano!" she said and dumped it.

I smiled, "I'll take that as a yes on the surf conversation."

Emma grinned, "OK."

༄ Chapter 21

I walked over to where Jessica was sitting. She was staring out at the ocean.

"How was breakfast?"

She'd been crying and she wiped her hand against her face.

I nodded, "It's not exactly your typical café, is it?"

She looked up at me and smiled as she wiped her hand against her cheek again, "No, it definitely isn't."

"You doing OK?"

She looked out at the ocean again, "I think so."

"Mind if I sit down?"

"Please," she replied and indicated toward the seat across from her.

I slid into it.

"What is this place?" she asked after a moment, then glanced back at the café.

"It's a strange, unusual, little spot which will probably change your life forever."

"Oh, so that explains it then," she replied and gave me a small smile.

We sat in silence for a few minutes.

"Who are you?" she asked.

"What do you mean?"

"Who are you? Casey mentioned that Mike owns this place. Emma told me he usually does the cooking too. So who are you? Do you really work here?"

I smiled, "Well...today I do."

She gave me a confused look.

"Do you want the long story or the short story?" I asked.

"How about you start," she replied, "and I'll ask for more details when I need them."

"Fair enough."

I took a moment to think. Where to start. How far back to go.

"About ten years ago, I visited this place," I began. "The café I mean." I didn't tell her it had been in an entirely different point geographically and somehow had been recreated in exact detail here in Hawaii. All without having aged a day. No point in making things even more confusing than they already were.

"At that time I was struggling to figure out my life."

"What do you mean? Were you unhappy?"

"Not *unhappy* exactly. I just wasn't *happy*. It felt like I was stuck on 'OK'. My job was OK, my activities outside of work were OK, my relationships were OK. And something inside kept telling me that life was supposed to more than just OK.

"Then there were a series of events which really made me think."

Jessica looked at me, "What happened?"

"I was sitting in my apartment one night and got a call from my family. They told me my eighty-two year old grandfather had just died."

"I'm sorry."

"Thanks. It's a long time ago now. The thing is, I wasn't even very close to him. Our family lived far away from my grandparents, and so even though he was my grandfather, I didn't really know him well. For some reason though, his passing shook me up. After I hung up that call, I looked at my life. And I thought, 'If I keep living this life, if I keep walking this path...'"

"Will I be happy at eighty-two?" Jessica added.

I nodded my head, "Exactly. And the answer was no. I wouldn't be happy. I'd just be OK. For some reason, in the instant I knew the answer was no, I remembered something which happened to me about five years earlier.

"Back then I'd just graduated college and was trying to enter the 'real world' of working. I got a call for a job interview. It was for a company in the downtown area of the big city near where I lived.

"So I got all dressed up in my suit, tie, starched shirt and uncomfortable shoes. Then I took my brand new computer bag, and got on the train heading into the city. I'd never ridden the train before, and when I got off the train, I accidentally turned the wrong way. Only it turned out to be exactly the right way."

"What do you mean?" Jessica asked.

"When I turned the wrong way, coming out of the train, I was standing and facing the mass of people who were leaving the train and walking toward the exit. Thousands of them all heading off to work. Old people, middle aged people, some just a few years older than me. And as I looked at that throng of men and women, I noticed something."

"What was it?"

"None of them were smiling. No one."

Jessica nodded.

"On that day, when I saw all those unhappy people, I vowed I wouldn't be like that. My life would be different."

Jessica nodded, "So you made it different?"

I shook my head, "Not really. That's what I realized the night I received the call about my grandfather. I'd wanted to do it differently. I'd vowed to do it differently. In reality though, there I was five years into things, and I realized my life wasn't very different."

"So what did you do?"

"I decided to take a trip to get away from it all for a little while. On the first night of the trip, through a series of very unusual events, I found myself hopelessly lost. And in the midst of being so lost, I wandered into a tiny little café with good food, nice people, and very unusual questions on the menu."

"You found this place," Jessica replied.

"Uh huh."

"And?"

"I spent all night in the café. Just talking to people. Mike, Casey, another woman who was there.... I listened to their stories. I shared my own story and what I was going through."

"Doesn't it seem odd you would have those kinds of conversations with strangers?"

I shrugged. "Yes, no, maybe.... I was at a point where I was no longer satisfied with 'OK'. That made me open to things I might not otherwise have been open to I guess."

I smiled, "Now I have conversations with strangers all the time. Once you try it, you realize it isn't so odd after all."

Jessica nodded, "What happened next?"

"That night at the café changed my life. I learned things I'd never realized before. I saw the world in a way I'd never seen it. I got a glimpse into a life which was more than just *OK*. So I decided to go live that life."

"And have you?"

I nodded, "I have."

ೲ Chapter 22

Mike took a bite of his french toast and nodded toward the patio, "John and Jessica seem to be getting along pretty well."

Emma took a sip of juice, "John is funny. He's nice too."

Casey ran her hand over Emma's hair, "Jessica is nice too."

"Why was she crying before?"

"She's forgotten how to play," Casey replied.

"Maybe you could help her remember," Mike said to Emma. "You're really good at playing."

"OK. What does she like to play?"

"I don't know exactly," Casey said. "I don't think she knows either. She did mention she used to like playing on the swings though."

"Maybe we can take her to the swings by the lagoon. Those are *awesome* swings. You can even twist and untwist them and then you spin around really really fast."

Mike smiled, "That sounds like a great idea. I think she'd like that."

"Can we go now?"

"Why don't you finish up your breakfast first. Then you and Casey can take her. I'll stay here with John and help clean up the kitchen."

"OK."

Emma took a few more bites of her pancakes. "Dad, I have a question."

"What is it?"

"How could anyone forget how to play?"

Mike smiled again. He was constantly in awe of how little kids could process things. They asked, they listened, they thought. Then when they didn't understand, they would ask again until they completely understood.

"I think in Jessica's case, she didn't have a very good family life when she was growing up," Casey said. "She didn't have someone like your Dad to teach her the joy of playing."

Emma thought for a moment, "That's sad."

"Yes it is," Casey replied.

"Do you think she can remember again?" Emma asked.

Casey smiled, "I think so. It's kind of like when you have a toy that you forget is under your bed, so you don't play with it for a long time. Eventually you don't even remember it's there. But when you find the toy, and start playing with it again, it all comes back to you. You remember how much fun the toy is."

"That happened with my stuffed dolphin one time," Emma replied excitedly. "His name is Dolphy. I lost him and looked everywhere but couldn't find him. I was really sad. Then I forgot about him until we moved things around to paint my room. It turns out Dolphy had been hiding behind my dresser *the whole time*! So now I play with him a lot again."

Casey smiled, "It's a lot like that. I think maybe if you take Jessica to the swings, she might begin to remember how fun it is to play again."

"Hey, it worked with Dolphy!" Emma said enthusiastically.

৵ Chapter 23

Jessica and I were still talking. She took a sip from her cup, "What does that feel like?"

"What does what feel like?"

"Choosing a different life."

I smiled, "I highly recommend it. Especially if your life is just OK and you'd like it to be more than that."

Jessica smiled back.

"Why do you think you're back here?" she asked. "Why now? You've got things all figured out, right? You're beyond OK."

I nodded, "I'm definitely living a life beyond OK." I shrugged my shoulders, "I'm not sure why I'm here this time. Maybe to learn more? Maybe to share what I've learned already? I'm not sure."

"What can you share with me?"

I smiled, "What do you want to know?"

Jessica leaned forward a bit, "Casey sort of rocked my world a little while ago."

"I saw you were pretty emotional. What happened?"

Jessica explained the conversation she and Casey had, including the idea of the playground.

"I don't know why it hit me so hard when she was explaining it," she said.

"Probably because it relates to your life."

I saw a sadness sweep across Jessica's face.

"Tell me one of the things you've learned since you were here before," she said.

I laughed, "Just one?"

"Start with one."

I thought about it for a minute. "How about another train story?"

She smiled, "OK, another train story."

"When I left the café the first time, I realized I didn't want to keep living the same life I'd been living. I also didn't know what life I *did* want to live."

I looked down at the menu, "On my menu from before, some of the questions were different than these. I think maybe the questions are different for everyone."

Jessica nodded, "Casey mentioned something about that earlier today. I didn't know what she meant."

"I know," I said. "It probably doesn't make sense on a thousand traditional levels, but just roll with me on this. On my menu, the first question was 'Why are you here?'"

"That's the same question on my menu," Jessica said. "I wasn't sure what it meant."

"I wasn't sure either when I first came into the café. Over time it became clear. It's not asking why are you in the café, or why are you in Hawaii.... It's asking why do you exist? Why are you alive? What is your PFE, which means Purpose for Existing?"

Jessica leaned back in her seat, "And I thought the playground question was out there."

"Right. Well, it's not really that far out there when it starts to sink in. Because what I realized was if I asked that question of myself—Why am I here?—my answer would be a good guide for what to do every day. Or so it seemed anyway."

"What do you mean?"

"Because of where I was at in my life, it was too big for me. I couldn't get my arms around it."

"So you got on a train?"

I laughed, "Yes. To go to work. I would think about that first question all the time. Especially while heading to my job. Then one day I met this guy on the train. Just a random guy on a random train ride into work."

"And?"

"He seemed happy. Genuinely, legitimately happy. So I said to him, 'I know this might sound crazy, but you seem happy, what's your secret?'"

Jessica laughed, "You really did that?"

I nodded.

"What did he say?"

"First he asked me about my life. I told him about what I was going through, about visiting the café, and about wanting more than OK."

"Did he think the café story was strange?"

I shook my head, "No. I think he lived in a mind space where the right things happen when they're supposed to. And the right people cross your path when you need them most. So my café experience made sense to him."

"Then what happened?"

"He told me two things in particular which got me jump started. The first was that he made his living by traveling the world and teaching different courses. That immediately caught my interest. I'd always wanted to travel the world, but didn't know anyone who had ever done it.

"Then he told me he himself had experienced a similar time in his life, when he was trying to figure things out."

"What did he do to get clear?"

"Apparently, a good friend helped him out a lot. I think his friend's name was Thomas. He inspired this guy to think about the five things he most wanted to do, see, or experience in his life before he died. Then focus his time and energy on those first. The rest would follow. He called them his Big Five for Life.

"He said sometimes the idea of figuring out your purpose in life is too overwhelming. So you start smaller, with these five things. Then as you are out there doing those, you get to know *you*. Once you know *you* better, it's easier to get clear about your purpose."

"Do you stay in touch with this guy?"

I smiled, "Nope. That's what was so strange. I only met him that one time on the train. He shared that concept with me on a day when I really needed it. And I never saw him again. Now in my memory files he's just, Joe. Joe from the train."

"Did you take his advice?"

"I did. I decided one of my five things was to travel. So I saved for two years and then started traveling the world. I loved it. As a matter of fact, I loved it so much I started alternating between a year of travel and a year of work. Then another year of travel and another year of work. I've been doing it ever since."

"Aren't you worried you won't be able to find a job when you come back?"

"I was at the start. Not anymore. Most people don't like their work, so they end up doing a pretty poor job at it. Which means if you're the type of person who really gives it your all, you stand out and then lots of people want to hire you."

"Even for a year?"

"Well, at the start I didn't tell people I was just going to be there for a year. Now though, I keep getting hired back by the same companies I've worked for in the past. They know I do a good job, so they can't wait for me to come back."

I shrugged, "Every company has a special project or two they would love to get done. They just don't have someone available who can make it happen. And they don't want to hire someone for that project only. They love that I come in, take care of it, and I'm not looking for a permanent job."

"Are you going to do this forever? One year of work, one of travel?"

"I don't know. So far it works for me. The first time was the toughest. What to do with my stuff, how to pay bills while I'm gone.... Once you figure out those types of things, it's really easy. I guess if I get tired of it at some point, I'll stop. For now though, it's..."

"Way better than OK?" Jessica asked.

I laughed, "Yes, definitely way better than OK."

Jessica looked out at the ocean.

"What is it?" I asked.

"You make it sound so easy."

"It is easy."

"For you."

"For anyone."

"But what if you've got a family? You can't just get up and go like that."

"Do you have a family?"

"No."

"Then why are you worried about it?"

"I'm just saying. It's not like everyone can go off like that."

"But why are *you* worried about it?"

She paused, "I don't know."

I smiled, "The days are too short to figure out your life by analyzing what may or may not work for everyone else's. Keep the analysis to Jessica and Jessica's situation.

"And, to be completely clear, I've met all kinds of people and all kinds of families doing things just like what I do. It's just that the majority of people never meet them or hear their stories, because the majority of people are sitting at work. And those people are out traveling. It's only once you get out and start traveling too, that you figure out what's possible.

"Which coincidentally, is what I've discovered about most things. Almost everything seems new and strange until you start doing it. And the only way to start doing it, is to..."

"Start doing it," Jessica interjected.

"Exactly. Then it doesn't seem new or strange at all. Plus, that's where you meet other people who know a lot about it. If you want to learn ballroom dancing, don't hang out at the baseball stadium. If you want to learn baseball, don't hang out at the ballroom dancing studio."

Jessica laughed, "Tell me something else you've learned."

I thought for a moment, "You were talking about the playground, right?"

"Uh huh."

"Live *your* playground."

"What does that mean?"

"Is having a husband, two kids, and a house with a big yard, *your* playground? Or did you get that idea from a bank commercial? Is heading to the beach in a convertible with three friends, and you're all singing to the radio *your* playground? Or is that life through the lens of a car commercial you watched?"

I smiled, "Your playground is unique to you. Allow yourself to evaluate it not by how full it is of someone else's dreams. But how full it is of *your* dreams?"

೧ Chapter 24

"Do you like it, Jessica?" Emma asked.

She, Jessica, and Casey were in a grotto, a short distance from the café.

"It's beautiful," Jessica replied.

They'd walked there via a small path which was surrounded by giant tropical foliage. Now, they were all swinging on swings at the edge of a small, beautiful lagoon. The amazing fragrance of Hawaii was everywhere. Flowers, flowers, and more flowers.

In this area of the island, the black volcanic rock which made up so much of Hawaii's shore line, had been eroded away by ocean waves. The result was a tropical paradise within an already tropical paradise.

The lagoon was filled with ocean water so clear they could see the tropical fish swimming below. Deep green foliage from plants with leaves so large they were bigger than a person, surrounded the lagoon. And the black volcanic rock that made up the edge of the lagoon, completed the picture.

"This is one of my favorite places to swing," Emma said. She was lying on her stomach on her swing, and spinning until the ropes twisted up tight.

"Watch this," she said.

She lifted her feet off the ground and the ropes began untwisting, causing her to spin around and around.

"You can try it if you want," Emma said to Jessica. "It's really fun. And it's not too scary after you do it a few times."

Jessica smiled, "It does look like fun."

"Try it," Emma said again.

"Well, I'm not sure it will be as easy for me..."

"That's OK, you can just give it a try," Emma persisted.

Jessica hesitated, "OK," she said. She positioned herself on the swing, as Emma had done.

"You just twist yourself around until it's super tight, and then lift up your feet," Emma said.

Jessica followed the instructions. When she lifted up her feet, she twirled as Emma had.

"You did it!" Emma cheered. "I told you you could."

Jessica stood up, smiled, and sat back down on her swing. "You're a good coach, Emma."

"Well, Casey said you liked to swing on the swings when you were a kid, and that you sort of forgot. So I thought I would just help you remember."

Jessica smiled again, "Thank you."

"Hey, there's Sophia," Emma said and pointed.

A young girl who looked about Emma's age was coming across the lagoon on a paddle board.

"Sophia! Sophia!" Emma shouted and waved.

The girl on the paddle board heard the shouting and waved back.

"I'm going to go play in the tide pools with Sophia," Emma said and raced towards the water. "I'll either be there or here," she yelled over her shoulder.

"OK," Casey replied.

"Will she be alright?" Jessica asked.

"She'll be fine. Those two know every inch of this lagoon. Sometimes I think they're half fish or half sea turtle."

"What did she mean by 'there or here?'"

"She and Mike have an ongoing agreement. He's open to allowing her to explore with her friends. She just has to pick the areas where she'll be exploring and let him know."

"Isn't that dangerous?"

"No, it's actually the opposite. He started doing it when she was really small. Back then no matter where she picked to explore he'd make sure he could see her and get to her quickly. He taught her to trust her instincts and her intuition. It was good training. At this point, she has a finely tuned internal guidance system. It keeps her safe while she's exploring."

"It still seems a little dangerous."

"If you knew what was going to happen before it happened would the world seem dangerous?"

Jessica paused, "Are you telling me she has that ability?"

"Everyone has it. She's been taught to use hers from a young age, so it's second nature to her. For most people, they stop pretty early in life. So when it pops up, instead of it being second nature, they second guess it."

"I see."

Casey could sense the doubt in Jessica.

"You used yours today."

Jessica looked at her quizzically.

"You came into the café this morning even when there was no rational reason to. Something spoke to you though. In some way, shape, or form, your internal guidance system gave you a clue that it was the right thing to do."

"How did you know that?"

Casey looked out at the lagoon and smiled, "That's how everyone finds the café."

ༀ Chapter 25

"You have an amazing daughter, Mike."

Mike and I were cleaning things up in the kitchen.

He smiled, "Thanks. She's a great kid."

"Do you like being a Dad?"

Mike put down the plates he'd been carrying, "Best thing ever...*for me*."

I smiled, "That was a heavy emphasis on the *for me*."

"Being a parent isn't for everyone. If it's your thing, it's a ton of fun and a lot of responsibility. If it's not your thing, it's a ton of work and a lot of responsibility."

"I don't think I've ever heard anyone say that."

He smiled, "That's because once you have kids you can't give them back."

"So it's not for everyone, huh?"

"No. Definitely not. And that doesn't mean someone is a better or worse person because they do or don't have kids. Just that it's not the right fit for everyone."

"What makes it a good fit for you?"

"By the time I had Emma, I'd already taken care of the most challenging person possible."

I laughed, "Who's that?"

"Me."

"You?"

"Parenting is a lot about giving. Not too many people are honest about that. On the commercials you see this adorable little baby cuddling on their parent's shoulder. Or the perfect little family moment where everyone is fresh and smiling and the child is doing some incredibly cute thing. The commercials show the getting. The transfer of love from the child to the parent."

"That's not it, huh?"

"That is it—sometimes. And a lot of times it's changing diapers, getting your child dressed, preparing their food, comforting them when they're crying, helping them get to sleep, teaching them things you already know.... Especially when children are young—parenting is a lot about giving."

He paused, "A lot of people have a child because they want to receive. For them, they feel disillusioned after a while."

"Not you?"

"Well, like I said, by the time I had Emma, I'd taken care of *me* already. I'd seen the things I wanted to see. I'd gone off on the adventures I wanted to have.... I was ready to give."

"Is there any receiving?"

"Tons. Every day. It's in small ways though. I'd never changed a single diaper before Emma was born. Had no clue how to do it, and pretty much was expecting the worst. Then she arrived and here is this little tiny person who needs your help. She can't do it on her own. So you help, and it makes you feel good. You receive."

I smiled, "I never thought diaper changing was anything but diaper changing. Although to be honest, I've never changed one."

Mike nodded, "When you've taken care of your own needs already, then when the child arrives, you can see them for the gift they are. They're a tiny person who is giving you the chance to help them. Changing a diaper isn't a responsibility—it's a chance to give a gift."

Mike laughed, "Which you give about ten times a day when they're really little."

"So you receive because you give?"

"Exactly. The joy comes from helping. Some people aren't ready for that. They're in a place where they want to receive first, then maybe give. That's not the way it works with parenting."

"And yet you said it's the best thing ever."

Mike nodded, "For me."

He hung up the dishtowel he'd been using to dry the dishes. "There's only so much time each day, John. Even before they have kids, most people are running around crazy busy. Something has to give when the child arrives. Because more than anything else, what the child really needs is time, love, and attention."

Mike paused, "Do you remember from last time you were here, the concept of PFE?"

"Sure, Purpose for Existing. I was just talking about that with Jessica."

"Perfect. Well, if someone has figured out their PFE and in order to live that purpose, it means their life is non-stop busy with their career..." he paused. "How are they going to fit in time, love, and attention for a child?"

"So maybe their Purpose for Existing doesn't include being a parent," I said.

"Exactly. Or maybe it doesn't include it right now. So they shouldn't feel bad about it, or pressured from their friends, family, or society. They're fulfilling their PFE in a different way.

"I've met a lot of customers here at the café who want to have a child because they want a 'full' life. That's a myth. Because having a child makes the child part full, but it means another part is not as full. Maybe you don't inspire as many people, or come up with as many inventions, or grow your business as big....

"The point is, John, each person is different, and unique, and special. Their Purpose for Existing may or may not involve being a parent and everything that entails. And that's fine."

"It doesn't seem so fine out there," I replied, "In the outside world."

"I know. Especially for women. But the truth is, if having a child was the key to incredible peace, contentment, and happiness, you'd see a lot more peaceful, content, and happy adults."

"And yet you said it's the best thing ever."

"Because it's part of my PFE. And I was at the point where I was ready to be there for Emma, not ask her to fill *my* emotional tank."

৩৩ **Chapter 26**

"It looks like they're having a good time," Jessica said and indicated towards Emma and Sophia.

"Always," Casey replied. "They have very similar playgrounds and they love playing in them together."

"What do you mean?"

"They like the same things. They're both crazy about the water. They love animals. They live for things like snorkeling, paddle boarding, surfing…"

"And apparently checking out tide pools," Jessica added.

Casey smiled, "That too."

They were silent for a while.

"I had a friend like that once," Jessica finally said.

"When you were little?"

"No. When I was twelve. Ashley Jessins. Her family moved in down the street from where I lived. We used to do everything together."

"Are you still in touch with her?"

Jessica shook her head, "No. When I decided to leave, I ran as far and as fast as I could."

"Are you still running?"

Jessica stopped swinging, "What do you mean?"

"Are you still running?"

Jessica thought for a minute, "I don't know. I'm certainly not that kid anymore. I have a career, and a life..."

"That doesn't mean you aren't running," Casey said. "When things are bad, we leave. We run. That takes courage. To get out of a situation which isn't what you want, especially one where you get hurt every day... that's brave."

Jessica nodded.

"Sometimes we get so used to running away though, we forget to stop running from and start running *toward*."

"I don't follow you."

"You're a long way from the mainland. That life you were running from back there happened a long time ago. But it's still a big part of you. Isn't it? What you do, the things you think about.... You're still trying to run from it."

A tear rolled down Jessica's face. "You don't understand," she said. "It was bad." She wiped the tear away, but more flowed, "It was very bad."

Casey nodded, "It isn't anymore though." She reached out and put her hand on Jessica's, "Maybe it's time to stop putting so much time and energy and emotion into running away from a life you didn't create. And instead apply those toward creating a life you *do*."

Casey released Jessica's hand, "Do you work?"

Jessica nodded.

"You have a very nice car, and very expensive clothes, and the latest phone.... I ask this not in judgement, but from a place of pure openness. Why?"

Jessica turned in her swing. She hesitated.

"I'm not saying there's anything wrong with it," Casey said. "Those things are all very nice. I'm just asking why do *you* own them?"

"I want to prove I belong," Jessica replied after a long pause. "I want to prove I belong."

"To what?"

Jessica shook her head and laughed in spite of herself, "I don't know. I guess I just don't want people to see me for what I used to be, for where I came from."

Casey nodded, "Who are you really?"

"What do you mean?"

"Some people love cars. They love the way it feels to sit in a new car. They love the engineering and the hum of the engine when they push the accelerator. They appreciate the symmetry of the design and the beauty of a car. Is that you?"

Jessica shook her head, "No."

"Some people love clothes. They get excited by the latest styles and admire the creativity of the designers. They can identify the nuances that make each piece of clothing unique and special. They love the way a particular item makes them feel. Is that you?"

Jessica shook her head, "No."

Casey smiled, "Sometimes, without our realizing it, we try to prove to the world that we belong. At the start it's about wanting other people to like us or recognize us, or see value in us. Then at some point we realize the truth. We're trying to belong to a club we don't really want to be in.

"What we do really want, more than anything else, is to be accepted into our own club. Yes we want to be validated. But in our heart of hearts, we're not waiting for someone else to say we're special. We're wanting for us to acknowledge to ourselves that *we're* special. And when we do that, the need for everyone else's validation slips away. We know we're special— all on our own."

Jessica nodded.

"What made you come here?" Casey asked. "To Hawaii."

"I wanted to learn how to surf."

"Really?"

Jessica nodded, "I saw this movie one time about a surfer. And he talked about how free it felt to ride the waves. And how when you were out surfing, the whole world disappeared. All you felt was the waves, the board, and this sense of harmony...." She shrugged, "Stupid I guess."

"Do you surf?"

Jessica shook her head, "No. When I got here everything was so expensive. I didn't have much money, so I took a job right away to pay for my rent and food. I still couldn't make ends meet, so I took another job at night. Then...I don't know. It just seemed foolish at some point."

"Surfing?"

"Just the whole idea that it could mean freedom and harmony and all that...."

"Are you still poor?"

Jessica shook her head again, "No. I mean I'm not rich, but I'm not poor by any means."

Casey smiled, "I'm still not clear who you are?"

Jessica smiled back, "What do you mean?"

"Well, you're not the clothes you wear. You're not the car you drive. You're not the girl who ran away from a tough upbringing. You're not the poor girl who first came here.... So who are you?"

The smile faded from Jessica's face, "I don't know."

Casey nodded, "That's why you're still running away from, instead of running toward."

༺ Chapter 27

Mike and I were still in the kitchen, cleaning up and talking.

He laughed, "We've covered a lot of ground on the topic of parenting, John. Any news you'd like to share?"

"Oh, no. I...I..." I smiled, "I don't know really. The last bunch of years have been amazing. *Really* amazing. I'm so glad I found this place the first time. It changed my life. And I want to thank you for that."

Mike nodded.

"And now I'm back here and I'm not sure why?"

"Why do you think?"

"I don't know. I assume there's something else for me to learn, or an area for me to grow...."

Mike smiled, "Maybe. Or maybe this time you're here to teach."

"To Jessica?"

"Possibly. Or to Casey, or Emma, or me."

I laughed, "I'm not sure there's much I could teach you which you don't already know."

"Don't be so sure. You've been living an amazing life since you were here last time. I'm sure you've learned a lot along the way."

I nodded, "I have. And I'm much more comfortable with my life, and my role in the greater picture, but..."

"But, who am I to...," Mike said.

I shrugged, "Sort of."

"John, the first phase is getting comfortable enough with yourself, that *you* believe in *you*. You get clear about your Purpose for Existing and start to live it. You've done that. You've gone beyond that.

"At some point, everyone on that path realizes most of our growth happens through inspired moments with others. Someone says something you never forget. Someone teaches you a concept you use for the rest of your life.

"As that's happening, you also start to see that the more in line you are with your PFE, and the more you live it every moment of every day, the more people are drawn to you. You glow with an energy that can't be faked. Your authenticity and clarity attracts those around you.

"At some point, it could be a random conversation, or an exchange with a friend who comes to you for advice, you share what you know with someone else. And you see the way it changes their life. Just like your life was changed when someone shared with you.

"And in that moment, you come to one of the great realizations. The question is not, who am I to teach, share, make a difference, start a business, travel the world, fall in love, write a song..., or insert any other dream of choice. The question is—who are you not to?"

ꙮ Chapter 28

Casey smiled at Jessica, "Have you ever used a GPS driving device? The kind where it automatically knows where you are? Then you type in where you want to go, and in a very friendly voice it guides you there?"

Jessica laughed in spite of herself, "Yes."

"I've found that's the way the universe works."

"What do you mean?"

"We make decisions in life. We try things. We turn left, we turn right." Casey laughed, "We go in circles."

Jessica smiled.

"And sometimes, it feels like we're so far off course that no-one or nothing could ever get us back." Casey looked at Jessica, "Do you know what I mean?"

Jessica nodded.

"But think about the GPS device. No matter how many times you go in circles, doing the same thing, making the same mistakes.... No matter how many times you go left when the little voice was telling you to go right.... With complete non-judgement, the voice comes on, says, 'recalculating' and then gives you everything you need to get where you want to go."

Jessica laughed, "It does, doesn't it?"

"It does," Casey replied. "And the universe works the same way." She stopped swinging and looked at Jessica, "You are here for something important. Your life is not a mistake, or an accident, or a random act of coincidence. You have a purpose, or you wouldn't be here. And although at times it may feel like you are hopelessly lost and could never find your way out, help is always there."

Something in Casey's story had touched a nerve.

"There have been times when I felt like I was so far off the map," Jessica began quietly. "Even now, many days I just feel...so lost."

Casey smiled, "Time to call on the universal GPS." She looked at Jessica, "Do you like the word God?"

Jessica gave her a quizzical look, "Do I like the word *God?*"

"Uh huh."

"I don't know. Why?"

"Some people like that term. It works better for them than universe."

"Does it matter?"

"That depends on you. While we're talking, I'll use universe. That's kind of a general term. After you've had a chance to think about it, you can pick whichever word you like best. There are lots to choose from. People from different places, with different backgrounds, and who speak different languages, use different words. The same words have changed over time too, so there's a whole history of words you can pick from."

"Is one better than the other?"

Casey smiled, "To some people."

"What about to you?"

"The essence of what we're talking about is a presence so powerful that it's a piece of every living thing. Not just here on our planet, but everywhere as far into the depths of space as there is space. And it exists not just now, but as far back as there has been far back." Casey smiled, "From my perspective, it's a little hard to believe something that powerful, would get caught up in a name. I think it's more the intention behind the inquiry that matters."

Jessica nodded, "How do you use this universal GPS?"

"That also depends."

"On what?"

"How lost you are." Casey looked out across the lagoon, "Do you remember the first question from the café menu?"

Jessica nodded, "Why are you here?"

Casey smiled, "Uh huh." She said nothing more.

"What is it?"

"What's the first step when you use a driving GPS?"

"Turn it on."

Casey laughed, "OK, birth. What's the next step."

Jessica thought for a moment, "The GPS figures out where you are."

"This one knows all the time. Next step?"

"Type in where you want to go."

Casey nodded, "Answering for yourself that question—*Why am I here?* Or stated another way, what is my purpose, which at the café we call PFE, Purpose for

Existing. That's the equivalent of telling the universe, 'this is where I want to go.'"

Jessica thought for a few moments, "That seems overwhelming. How do I know what my purpose is?"

"Use the search option."

"The what?"

"You know. On the GPS there are search options. If you don't know exactly where you want to go, you can look for a theme. 'Italian Restaurants', 'Places of Interest', 'National Parks...'"

Jessica laughed.

"It's true," Casey said and smiled. "Life works the same way."

"I get it but I don't get it."

"OK. Imagine you're driving. You've been driving for a while. What happens to make you stop driving?"

Jessica thought for a minute, "I'm tired of driving?"

"Good. Then what?"

"I decide to stop?"

"Right, but what happens before that?"

Jessica looked confused.

"Just think about it for a minute," Casey said. "What happens right before you decide to stop?"

"I think of something. I think of something I want to do more than driving. A thought, or an idea will pop into my head and that's my clue," Jessica said excitedly.

Casey nodded, "Same thing here. Every second of every day, we are getting clues. Someone like John mentions traveling around the world like he's done. Either we have no interest in doing something like that, or something inside us says, *'Stop driving, let's go there! We've always wanted to do that! Why aren't we doing that now?'*"

"So is that a theme, or a specific destination?"

"That depends on the person. Maybe it's not your Purpose for Existing exactly, but somehow, some way, it's really important."

Jessica nodded, "When John and I were talking, he told me the concept of PFE was overwhelming for him at first. So he started with the five things he most wanted to do in his life. He said it was easier for him to grasp that. Then as he was out doing those, his purpose became clear."

Casey nodded, "For some people that's a great way to get started."

"And for other people?"

"Some are born with an innate sense of their purpose. They've known it for as long as they can remember." Casey paused, "I'll share this with you too. The universal GPS and the driving GPS share one other feature."

"What's that."

"They watch you. And based on what they see, they change what they give you."

༻ Chapter 29

I went over to a counter in the corner of the kitchen and grabbed my backpack.

"Leaving so soon?" Mike asked and smiled.

I smiled back, "*Who am I not to.* I want to capture that before I forget it."

I unzipped the backpack and brought out my notebook of 'ahas!'.

"What's that for?" Mike asked.

"Moments like these," I replied and wrote a note to myself on one of the empty pages. "When I left here last time, my mind was so full of thoughts and ideas and insights.... I knew if I didn't write them down, I'd forget some of them. So that night after I left, as soon as I found the gas station you told me about, I bought a little booklet and began capturing my 'aha!' realizations."

"How do you decide what's an *'aha!'*?"

"I just know. It's something where I shift instantly when I hear it. Sometimes they're small things, like a cool piece of information or a quote. Mostly though they're great pieces of life wisdom. Like what you just shared. When I hear them I know if I remember them, and apply the wisdom where appropriate, my life will change in a good way."

"So you write them down?"

I nodded.

"What do you do with them?"

"I flip through them at night right before I go to bed. Or if I'm having a tough day I'll pick up the notebook, select a random page, and start reading. It centers me. Keeps me inspired."

Mike smiled, "I like that. Can I see?"

"Sure." I flipped the book to him. He opened to a random page and read out loud.

"I can never lose this. Not a moment of it. Now that I have lived it, it is mine forever."

Mike smiled, "What does that refer to?"

"One morning when I was in the midst of my first year of traveling, I had a pretty powerful epiphany. So much of what we think we own is very illusory. Things break, they lose their value, someone steals them....

"Experiences though are yours to keep forever. Once you have them, no one can ever take them away. You don't have to keep paying taxes in order to keep them, like on a house. You don't have to put them under lock and key like gold or gems. They're yours. And you get to relive them again and again as many times as you wish, from anywhere in the world.

"That 'aha!' you just read left a powerful impression on me. It really changed much of my thinking about what I wanted to do with the money I earned. 'Things' became less important. Experiences took precedent."

Mike nodded, "I really like that. Funny I happened to flip to that particular 'aha!'. Just the other day one of our customers was sharing some information which would further support your epiphany."

"Which was?"

"Almost one out of five men never makes it to retirement age."

"You're kidding!"

"Nope. Almost twenty percent of men die before they turn sixty-five."

"That's incredible. And not in a good way. How could I have never heard that before?" I held out my hand, "Can I have my book back? That's an 'aha!' I want to capture."

Mike smiled and flipped me the book. "What a bad deal for all those men who save and save and save for retirement and then never get to reap the benefits."

"No kidding," I replied. I quickly wrote the 'aha!' in my notebook, then looked up, "Did your customer have any other bits of wisdom?"

"He did. He was called to do a television interview to talk about what to do with your tax refund. Should you save it or spend it? So he did some calculations about what the real decision was."

"Wasn't it a decision to save or spend?"

"Kind of. Although like you discovered with your 'aha!', spending can mean lots of different things. He wanted to come up with an example of what it would mean in terms of experiences."

"And?"

"Pretty amazing. He ran the analysis with the assumption that the tax refund was worth five thousand dollars. So the question was, spend the five thousand or save it for retirement?

"He gathered all the historical data for the stock market. Then he adjusted things for historical inflation and calculated what the actual value of the five thousand would be in the future. The guy is forty-two years old now, so the money would have twenty-three more years to grow before he hit retirement age."

"What did the results show?"

"Well, as you might expect, if he saved the money, it grew in value. He ended up having more to spend when he retired." Mike paused, "But it wasn't quite worth it when he looked at it from an experience perspective."

"Why not?"

"Well, as he explained in the television interview, he realized that his decision was this. He could take his wife and two teenage kids on a three week driving trip to see the Rocky Mountains this year. They could go hiking, fishing, white water rafting, bungee jumping, mountain biking, and a host of other activities.

"All of which would be great family time and create lots of wonderful memories. Which, per your 'aha!', are yours forever."

Mike paused and took a drink of water, "Or he could save the money and let it grow in value. Twenty-three years later, it would have grown enough so he could take two of those trips."

"Only his kids wouldn't be teenagers anymore," I said. "And he would miss out on twenty-three years of laughter and smiles every time he thought of the trip. Not to mention it's a little easier to do white water rafting, bungee jumping and all the rest of that at forty-two than it is at sixty-five."

"Especially if you're one out of the five men who doesn't make it to sixty-five," Mike added.

"No kidding," I replied. "Wow. When you look at it that way, choosing to not have that experience now seems like a horrible trade." I looked at Mike incredulously, "Are you sure your customer was right about the numbers?"

Mike nodded, "I know he is. He walked me through it in detail." He smiled again, "In addition to being a café customer, he's also my financial planner. He's a whiz with the numbers."

"So he told that story during the television interview?"

"He did. He explained he wasn't suggesting people shouldn't save. He's a big fan of having at least six months to a year's worth of income in savings. He also wasn't discouraging people from investing for retirement.

"As he put it though, be aware what your real decisions in life are. Most people work to make money. So invest it in ways that produce the 'real return' you're looking for. In his example, the real return of a fantastic three week vacation full of great family experiences, which become great family memories, had a specific value. A value more important to him than the possible chance for two of those vacations twenty-three years later."

⌀ Chapter 30

Jessica gave Casey a confused look, "The universe and the GPS are watching?"

"Uh huh."

"In what way?"

"The new GPS devices have technology which uses algorithms to analyze your behavior. For example, if you often have Italian Restaurants as your destination, it will start to give you Italian Restaurant listings even without you asking for them.

"Or if it's not Italian restaurants, maybe it's national parks, or waterfalls, or shopping malls. It watches for whatever you spend your time on and then gives you the chance to spend more time on those things."

"And you're saying the universe does that?" Jessica asked.

"It does. You see, the universe is not just listening. It's watching."

"Which means?"

Casey smiled, "Which means when someone says they want a different life. More freedom, a more pleasant environment.... But then they spend forty or fifty hours per week in a small cubicle working for a boss who treats them poorly..."

"Just like the GPS, the universe gives them more of what they seem to really like," Jessica said.

"Exactly. It's almost as if the universe says, 'Wow, look how often she spends her time there! She must LOVE IT! Let me give her even more of that.'"

Casey's voice became more subdued, "It's not just about work either. The universe watches everything. The types of relationships we put our time and energy into, the types of thoughts we dwell on.... Even the experiences we engage in which drive those thoughts."

"It almost sounds vindictive," Jessica said.

Casey shook her head, "I see how it might seem that way. It's not vindictive though. It's based on a simple premise. We are creatures of free will. We choose what we do, how we do it, where we spend our time, who we hang out with.... Logically, we would choose activities which bring us positive emotions—joy, love, contentment, happiness, excitement....

"So instead of being vindictive, the universe is actually an incredibly giving presence. Based on our actions, our thoughts, our intentions, it delivers exactly what we are demonstrating we want."

A shudder went through Jessica. Casey saw her reaction.

"Are you OK?"

Jessica nodded, "That's powerful."

Casey nodded too, "Isn't it? To realize that at anytime we have access to this incredible guiding system. And that no matter how far off we feel, it can guide us back on course. To also realize that the guiding system is being guided by *us*. It is responding to *our* actions, which means we're not just an actor in the play...we're the director too."

Jessica looked at Casey, "How do I get connected to this?"

"You already are. You can't disconnect. Every moment is being co-created by you and this guiding force.

You demonstrate what you want, the universal GPS creates opportunities in line with that."

"But I don't like my connection. I want to make it stop giving me the types of opportunities I'm getting."

Casey smiled, "Type in a new destination. Start demonstrating to the universal GPS your new preferences."

"It's that easy?"

Casey nodded, "It's that easy."

Jessica thought for a few moments. "How long does it take to start giving me new opportunities?"

"That depends. How clear of a signal are you going to send about what you really want? When people say they want to leave a toxic relationship, but then keep going back to it, the message they are really sending is—*I want more toxic relationship moments.*

"It doesn't matter what they say. It matters what they do. Just like with the driving GPS, each of us has built up a history. At the start, that history determines what we get offered. But when the algorithm sees we no longer request Italian Restaurants, and instead we're asking for Chinese..."

"It stops offering Italian and starts offering Chinese," Jessica said.

"Exactly. It's not trying to be vindictive. It's not like, 'Oh, let me see if I can convince them to eat Italian again tonight.'"

Jessica laughed, "The dark side of the GPS."

"Right. There is no dark side. It's learning, and offering, and adjusting based on us."

Jessica's eyes suddenly widened, "Can I delete?"

Casey smiled, "What do you mean?"

"On my car's GPS, I can delete my search history. I can clear out my fifty Italian restaurant requests. That way I start fresh. I don't have to go to fifty-one Chinese restaurants before it realizes I now want that more than I want Italian. The minute I go to one Chinese restaurant, it treats that as my new preference."

Jessica was excited. Casey could see it in her eyes.

"Can I do that?" Jessica asked.

Casey nodded, "Good for you, Jessica. You just figured out one of the most powerful parts of the universal GPS."

Jessica was beaming, "Perfect! How do I use it? How do I delete?"

"Make a change."

"No, but I don't want to just change. I want to delete my past. Just like on my driving GPS."

"It's not exactly the same, Jessica. Your past is your past. You can't totally delete it like that."

Jessica looked very sad all of a sudden. "But I thought you said I could? I thought you said I'd figured out one of the most powerful parts of the universal GPS?"

Chapter 31

I wrote a few more notes in my journal. "That's a great story, Mike. Your financial planner sounds like a really interesting guy. I'd like to meet him someday."

Mike nodded, "He is interesting. He looks at what he does in a way that's so different from most of his peers."

"He sounds very real," I replied. "No trying to cover things up, or make them seem like something they aren't."

"Which is why his business is so much more successful than his peers," Mike added. "And why he is so much happier than his peers, too. As he says, 'It's tough to be happy when you spend your day convincing people to do something you know isn't right for them.'"

Mike smiled, "He has this one other thing he does. Really powerful."

"What is it?"

"Let me think for a minute, so I get it right." Mike paused for a few seconds. "OK. Let's pretend you have a thousand dollars to invest."

"OK."

"In the first year you have a fifty percent loss on your investment."

"That doesn't sound good."

"But in the next year you have a fifty percent gain."

"I like that better," I said and smiled.

Mike smiled back, "What's your average return over the two years?"

I thought for a minute. "Let's see, down fifty percent the first year, up fifty percent the second year. My average return is zero."

"Correct. And how much money do you have at the end of the two years?"

"A thousand dollars. Since there was a zero percent return, I still have a thousand dollars." I paused for a minute. I knew that wasn't right. But it seemed right....

"Wow," I said after a minute. "It's not a thousand dollars. It's a lot *less* than a thousand dollars."

Mike nodded, "That momentary confusion you just had is the basis for one of the most interesting 'ahas!' my friend shares. You're right. It's not a thousand dollars. You start with a thousand and you lose fifty percent. Which means you are left with..."

"Five hundred dollars," I replied.

"Exactly. Then you gain fifty percent on that. So you have?"

"Seven hundred and fifty dollars," I replied. "That's horrible. I actually lost twenty five percent of my money, even though my average return for two years was zero!"

Mike nodded, "And yet what number does everyone quote when they talk about financial returns for investments?"

"Average return?"

Mike nodded again, "Exactly. And that's the kind of thing which really bothers my friend. It confuses people and it hides their true return. Because they get bad information, they make bad decisions, and then they don't really get to live the life they want to live.

"So he is all about breaking apart the myths so people can make good decisions. Decisions which enable them to fulfill their Purpose for Existing as much as possible."

I nodded, "Not to get too technical, but can I ask you a question?"

"Sure."

"If average return is a misleading number to use, what does your friend say is a better one?"

"Something called CAGR. It stands for compound average growth rate."

"My eyes are glossing over already," I said and smiled.

"The reality is simpler than the name," Mike replied. "It just means if you look at what you have at the start, and look at what you have at the end—what was your actual return on your money? You sort of already did it with our example from earlier."

"I did?"

"Uh huh. You realized that if we started with a thousand dollars, and after two years we ended up with seven hundred and fifty dollars, then we lost twenty five percent of our money. So the actual return is negative twenty five percent."

I wrote more notes in my 'ahas!' journal. "So if I want the truth, I should ask for what the actual return is, not the average return?"

Mike nodded again, "As my friend says, one is the truth, and one is a good way to hide the truth. Better to get the truth."

"That's kind of sad," I said.

"What's sad?"

"That people don't just tell it like it really is."

"That's one of the great adventures in life, John. Realizing that not everyone's moral compass points in the same direction. Then finding and filling your life with people whose morale compass is aligned with yours."

⌒ Chapter 32

"Your past is your past for a reason," Casey said. "If it wasn't for your past, this moment wouldn't be happening."

"But I don't like my past."

"That's OK. You don't have to like all of it. You also don't have to relive it. When you acknowledge the role it had in bringing you to right now...that's enough."

Casey looked at Jessica, "When we step back far enough, we see there is meaning in all things. It's a lot easier to do that when you know your new destination for the universal GPS. Once that's clear in your mind, you can see the ways different parts of your past have prepared you to get to this new destination.

"You see you weren't really lost that whole time. The universe was with you all the way. Helping you, guiding you, preparing you for the moment when you would choose your PFE and say, 'This is where I want to go.'"

"So I don't need to delete?"

Casey shook her head, "No."

"Why did you say it was so powerful then?"

"On the driving GPS, delete is powerful. It resets the computer and you start all over. In life, a dramatic shift does the same thing. It sends a very strong and clear signal to the universe to start recalibrating."

"How dramatic is dramatic?"

"That depends on the person. It might be ending a relationship. Or it might be the opposite—opening your heart and allowing a relationship to start. The more dramatic the change, and the more energy and time invested in the direction of the new change, the stronger and clearer the signal that's sent."

"And so the stronger the reset?" Jessica asked.

Casey nodded, "The stronger the reset. Demonstrate with intensity and clarity and conviction, and the universe responds in kind."

"It's hard to imagine."

"Think about your life up to this point. That's the simplest way to comprehend all of this. When you reflect on the ways in which your life has changed or not changed at different points, you'll find it all makes sense now."

Jessica let that sink in for a moment and then abruptly stood up.

"Are you OK?" Casey asked.

Jessica nodded and smiled. It was the most authentic smile Casey had seen her give yet. "I'm better than OK. I feel light somehow. Like...I don't know. This probably sounds crazy, but...like I can fly."

She looked toward Emma and Sophia playing in the tide pools. "I'll be right back," she said and kicked off her shoes.

"Where are you going?" Casey asked with a smile.

Jessica started running toward the girls. "I'm going to ask Emma if she'll teach me to surf," she called back.

ॐ Chapter 33

I heard the sound of their laughter before I saw Casey, Jessica, and Emma.

"Something good must have happened out there," I said to Mike. "There's an energy shift. I can hear it in their laughter."

Mike nodded and stood up from the stool he'd been sitting on, "Better start working on the surfboards. Going to need a couple of extra ones."

"Who's going...?" I started to ask, but Mike was already heading out the door.

"John! John! Do you want to come with us?"

It was Emma. She was running up the path. Her face filled with a giant smile.

I looked out through the serving window, "Hi Emma."

"Do you want to come with us?" she asked again. "We're going surfing. Jessica wants me to teach her. Do you want to come?"

I smiled. How had Mike known? "Absolutely," I said to Emma. "I'd love to."

Moments later, Jessica and Casey came up the path. There had definitely been an energy shift. Jessica looked so alive compared to this morning. She was smiling and laughing and looked excited. It was like she'd released a burden she'd been carrying and now was so light she could walk on air.

"Looks like your time at the swings was good," I said when they came up to the café.

Jessica nodded and smiled, "Life-changing good."

She put her arms up on the ledge, "We're going *surfing*," she said in a tone of voice I hadn't heard from her before. It, like her look now, was so full of energy, so full of life and fun.

"Are you coming, John?" Casey asked.

"I'd love to. As a matter of fact, I just told Emma I would." I glanced around the café, "If someone needs to stick around here though, I'm happy to take care of things."

"No need," Casey replied. She walked into the café and went to the area by the front door. I followed behind her. After searching through some items under the cash register, she pulled out a little placard with string attached.

"Perfect," she said.

"What is it?" I asked.

"A gift from one of our customers." She turned the plaque so I could see it. It was an oblong piece of flat driftwood. Written on it were the words—*Calling in well. Be back later.*

Casey hung it on the front door so the words faced out to anyone who came up to the café.

"What's 'Calling in well?'" I asked as we walked back into the kitchen.

"Isn't that a great expression?" she replied and started putting on sunscreen. "One of our customers taught it to me. He said most people are familiar with the idea of calling in sick. Basically, they tough it out through their life until they are so sick they're forced to give themselves a break. Then they spend the break recovering from what made them sick in the first place. Only to then return to that exact same thing.

"He said one of his greatest epiphanies was giving himself the gift of 'Calling in well,' now and again. So on some random day when his energy told him it was time, he would 'Call in well,' and go do one of the things he enjoyed most in life."

"That's a great expression," I replied. I reached for my 'ahas!' notebook and quickly jotted down—*allow yourself to call in well once in a while*.

Casey nodded toward my notebook, "Capturing some good ones today?"

"I am."

She closed the cap on the sunscreen and flipped it to me, "Let's go surfing."

೧೨ **Chapter 34**

I walked out of the bathroom and headed toward the back door. Jessica was just coming out of the ladies room.

"All set to surf?" I asked her.

She smiled, "Absolutely. I'm so happy I threw my bathing suit in the car this morning. It seemed crazy when the idea first came to me. Every time I tried to ignore it though, something kept telling me *TAKE IT!*" She laughed, "Now I see why."

"Perfect," I replied. I'd had a similar experience when I'd woken up. My plan was to take a bike ride, but something had told me the same thing—*take your swim shorts*. Now I too knew why.

We walked out the back of the café, onto the sand, and past the tables. Emma and Mike were already there. Mike had five surfboards leaning against a tree branch.

"Where's Casey?" Jessica asked.

"She'll be here," Emma replied. "She's a good surfer already, so she can skip the lesson."

Just then the back door of the café opened. I saw Casey. She had someone with her.

"Wow, that's bright," I said and shielded my eyes. It was like the sun had caught a glare all of a sudden and I could barely see Casey and the other person.

"You're not kidding," Jessica added. She shielded her eyes too.

"Dad, that's..." Emma began.

Mike smiled and bent down next to her, "Coconut, do you feel comfortable teaching Jessica? If you can do the land training, I'll go say hello to our customer. Then I'll come out and help with the water lessons."

"Sure," Emma replied. Mike squeezed her and kissed the top of her head, "Thanks, Coconut."

"Dad," Emma said when Mike stood up. "Dad."

Mike smiled, "What is it?"

Emma motioned for Mike to bend down. When he did, she whispered something into his ear. He smiled again, "OK," he replied.

With that, Emma sprinted toward the café. "Be right back," she called over her shoulder.

I held my hand up to my eyes to try and watch her. It was too bright though. I thought I saw Emma give the customer a hug, but it was so hard to see. As I tried to look, there was a brief moment when I sensed something very familiar about the customer. Then the light was too bright again, and I had to close my eyes for a minute.

"Jessica, this one's for you," Mike said. "John, why don't you give this one a try."

I turned away from the café and back towards the ocean. Mike was standing next to the surfboards and motioning towards two different ones.

Jessica and I walked to our boards.

"Jessica, have you ever surfed?" Mike asked.

"Never."

"Well then today will be the start of something amazing for you."

She smiled, "It sort of has been already."

Mike smiled back, "Even better. Well, we'll start with the basics here on the beach, including how to carry your board. Then we'll get you into the water and up riding some waves. Emma has a lot of experience on the waves. So do Casey and I. John's not far behind."

Mike was right. I didn't have a ton of experience, but I'd surfed a decent amount. I'd never told him that. But as with so many other things, he just seemed to know.

"So, holding the board..." Mike began.

"I got it. I got it, Dad," Emma said breathlessly.

We turned and saw her racing toward us.

"I got it."

Mike smiled, "In that case, I'm going to turn things over to one of our top instructors." He patted Emma on the head, "Call me if you need me. I'll meet you on the beach in a few minutes."

As Mike walked toward the café, Emma grabbed her board.

"You are going to LOVE surfing, Jessica!" she said, her voice full of excitement. "Before we get into the water though, it's important you understand the basics."

Emma placed her board on the sand, "OK, everyone grab your board and lay it gently on the sand next to mine."

Jessica and I put our boards down on the sand, facing the ocean.

"Surfing is a little about technique, a little about balance, and a lot about rhythm and energy," she said. "I'll show you the technique part here and the other parts we'll do in the water."

I smiled. How amazing that this little seven year old was so self-confident, and so comfortable with what she knew, that she could fearlessly teach it. And teach it to people decades older than her no less.

Over the next twenty minutes, Emma taught Jessica the basics of surfing. The way to carry the board. Getting beyond the break to calm waters. How to stand up on the board when she caught a wave. The right position for her feet and arms so she could keep her balance once she was up. The safest way to fall if she started falling off....

"The most common mistake people make is to try and stand up too early," Emma said. "Remember, when you start to feel the energy of the wave propelling you forward, keep paddling! That momentum is just the start of something amazing. When you feel it, dig deep with three good strokes of hard effort. Then stand up and enjoy the ride.

"If you try and stand up when you first feel the momentum, you aren't far enough into the energy of the wave yet. Your weight will be too much and you'll get behind the wave."

"What happens then?" Jessica asked.

"Well, you miss the wave. It rolls under you and you end up on the back side of it. Plus, and this is a big thing, all that initial energy you put in is lost. Because now you have to paddle back out beyond where the waves are breaking again. And when the waves are nice and big, that takes a lot of your time and energy."

Emma smiled and danced around a little, "You want to spend the day *surfing*, not paddling."

It was great advice. When I'd first learned to surf, no one had taught me about the three extra strokes. I'd spent an entire morning missing waves and exhausting myself just paddling back out beyond the break.

Jessica smiled, "OK coach. Let me re-cap what I do once I'm out there, just to make sure I've got this. First, I pick my wave. Once I do that, while I'm laying on the board, I use my arms to turn and position myself to catch the wave. Then I start paddling. When I feel the energy of the wave, I don't stop. I keep paddling for three more good strokes. Then I stand up and ride it in."

Emma was beaming, "Exactly! You totally have it, Jessica."

৩৩ **Chapter 35**

I smiled. Since my last visit to the café, there had been countless times when I'd realized how small lessons are so connected to big lessons. Hearing Emma teach Jessica about surfing, it struck me once again.

Everything she was sharing could be part of a course on life.

Pick a wave.

That's the same as pick where you want to go. It's your Purpose for Existing. Or in my case, my Big Five for Life, and then my PFE, since PFE was too much for me to wrap my mind around at the start.

Position yourself and your board to catch the wave.

That mirrors positioning yourself for living the life you want. Things like aligning your thoughts, emotions, and actions with your intentions. Spend in alignment with the life you want to live. Even physically putting yourself in the right place to have the experiences you want. Or putting yourself in the right environment or among the right people so you have the best chance for success.

Start paddling.

Take action. Begin the adventure. Try! So many times I'd met people with marvelous dreams. But they didn't take any action toward making those dreams a reality.

When you feel the energy of the wave, don't stop. Keep paddling for a few more strokes to get in flow.

How often I'd seen people give up just when they were poised to experience something amazing. Their fears would kick in, or they would get lazy in their actions or intentions. The flow was right there, but they stopped just short of it. Then they had to expend so much energy to start over again.

Ride the wave.

Enjoy! If all you do is paddle, paddle, and paddle some more, life gets boring. You burn yourself out. The point is not to always be getting ready to enjoy life, but to actually enjoy it. To ride the wave.

It was all there. So simple. So profound. And all taught by a seven year old.

"OK," Jessica said. "I'm ready. Let's hit the water."

"First we practice," Emma said and pointed toward the boards in the sand.

"In the sand?" Jessica asked surprised.

"Uh huh. We master the technique in a safe and easy environment like the sand. No waves to knock us over here. That way when we get to the water you'll already be comfortable with what to do and it won't scare you. OK, everybody on their board and get ready to paddle!" Emma said excitedly and laid down on her board.

I smiled and laid down on my board. "Another great life lesson," I thought to myself.

෴ Chapter 36

"Everyone ready to surf?"

It was Mike. He and Casey had their boards in hand and were walking towards us.

"Almost," Jessica said. She turned to Emma, "Can you show me that one more time?"

"Sure!" Emma coached Jessica through the process of pushing up on the board and getting to her feet. Then making sure her arms and legs were in the right positions to keep balanced.

"You're ready," Emma said. "Next stop, THE WAVES!"

She did a little dance in the sand.

Mike picked her up and turned her upside down, "Upside down surfing," he said.

Emma laughed and wiggled around.

"Again. Again," she said when he had put her down. "One more time."

He repeated it and she laughed even more.

"OK," he said after he'd put her down the second time. "Let's go!"

Emma led the way down to the beach. When she got to the edge of the water, she attached her surfboard ankle strap and waded in with her board.

"You OK?" Casey asked Jessica.

Jessica was fidgeting with her ankle strap and seemed a little hesitant.

"It was perfectly clear five minutes ago when we were up there." she replied. "I was totally ready to go. I was even thinking we should have just started in the water. Now here we are." Jessica looked out at the surf, "My heart is kind of pounding."

Casey smiled, "There's a very subtle difference between the feelings of fear and excitement," she said. "Sometimes when you haven't allowed yourself to be excited about life for a while, you forget the difference."

"I don't want to fall," Jessica said.

"That's part of learning to stand up," Casey replied and put her board into the water. "Come on. We'll be right with you the whole time."

Casey glanced at me. I smiled back.

"You can do it, Jessica," I said.

"Do you have any 'ahas!' for her, John?" Casey asked.

By now I was laying on my board and starting to gently paddle out. I turned a bit and smiled, "Every expert started off knowing nothing about what they became an expert in."

Jessica smiled. She put her board into the water and laid on it. "Time to start becoming an expert," she said and began paddling.

෴ **Chapter 37**

Mike and Emma were great teachers. They started Jessica off in the white water of the waves. Mike held the board for her and gave her a push at just the right time. Emma surfed alongside and watched for what she was doing right and wrong and then explained it to her.

Jessica fell the first four times. But then, on her fifth try, she stood up and rode her board all the way to shore. It wasn't the kind of ride that was going to make any surfing highlight reels. She wobbled, weaved, and almost fell, half a dozen times. But she had done it.

We cheered like crazy for her.

Little by little, wave by wave, she got more and more comfortable. She was beginning to become more of an expert. Soon, she didn't need Mike to give her a push. She had figured out the timing of the waves and could do it by herself. After a while, and all on her own, she decided she wanted to stop surfing the white water and started taking on small waves.

"She's doing really good!" Emma said excitedly. Emma had stayed with Jessica in the small waves for a while. Now she had paddled out just beyond the break to where Casey, Mike, and I were. Jessica was still close to shore.

"You're a really good coach, Emma," I said. "And it was really nice of you to stay with her in the small waves for so long. Especially when I hear you have no trouble with the big ones."

Emma shrugged, "That's how my Dad taught me."

"I'll tell you what, Coconut," Mike said and tapped Emma's board. "I'll head in and watch out for Jessica if you want to surf the big waves with John and Casey for a while."

Emma nodded, "OK."

"Can you keep on eye on her?" he asked us and motioned toward Emma.

"No problem," I said. "I'm mostly relaxing out here anyway."

Mike nodded, "Call me if you need me, Coconut." Then he turned his board toward shore and started paddling in to Jessica.

"Big waves coming," Emma said.

I looked behind us. There was a great set of waves approaching.

"All yours," I said and smiled. "My shoulders need a little rest."

I sat up and straddled my board. Casey did the same. Emma turned and started to paddle. The large wave came underneath us and for a moment we couldn't see Emma. I knew from experience she was paddling like crazy on the other side of the wave. In a moment, we saw her up on her board, surfing.

"She's good," I said.

Casey nodded, "Mike had her up on a board when she was three. At four she was surfing white water. By five she was taking on pretty big waves."

"I guess she loves it."

"That she does."

I looked toward shore and saw Mike surfing alongside Jessica. "How's Jessica doing?"

Casey smiled, "You mean aside from surfing?"

I nodded.

"She'll get there. She's fighting some inner demons. Beliefs about who she is and what she has to offer. She'll get there though." Casey turned to me, "And how are you?"

I held out my arms, "Hard to be anything but great when you're out here doing this. It's a very good channel."

"A what?"

I smiled, "A very good channel."

She smiled back, "And what does that mean in the context of being out here?"

"One day I was sitting in an outdoor café. I'd just about saved up enough money to head out traveling again, and I was working on my list of things to bring with. At the table next to me, two people were discussing all the things wrong with the world.

"It was the government, and the education system, how people are abusing unemployment benefits, the decline of the stock market.... You name it and they were focusing on it. Somehow as I sat there, I suddenly had this tremendous 'aha!'."

"Which you wrote in your book of 'ahas!'."

I smiled, "Yes I did."

"And what was the 'aha!'?"

"Think of life like one hundred television channels. Comedies, dramas, current events, reality cooking shows, news, sports.... The list goes on and on. Some of the channels you love. Others you like. Some you kind of like. And three of the channels are *really* annoying to you. To the point of being completely distasteful. You can't believe the programs are allowed to be on television.

"My 'aha!' was that many people spend their life watching the three channels they find really annoying. They stumble upon them at first. And they find them so unpleasant, so insulting on some level, that they feel compelled to tell everyone else about them.

"It's the opening part of all their discussions. 'Did you hear about...? Isn't it horrible how *this* happened, or *that* person was just caught doing...?' And just to keep proving to themselves how horrible the channels are..."

"They watch them all the time," Casey added.

I nodded, "Exactly! It becomes all consuming for them. They get so caught up in the three channels they dislike so much, they stop watching the other ninety seven channels. Over time, they completely stop thinking about the other ninety-seven channels. Eventually, they forget the other channels even exist."

"So this," Casey said and indicated toward the sun and the ocean, "is a good channel."

"An incredible one," I replied. "Now I'm sure at this very moment, there's someone out in the world doing something I'd find distasteful. And I could be mentally focusing on how wrong or unfair or selfish it is. But then I'd be missing all of this."

"So you tune out the channels you don't like?"

"Exactly. And the amazing thing is, over time, I forget those channels even exist. I so infrequently come into contact with them, it's like those channels aren't even on."

Casey smiled, "What do people who have become obsessed with the three channels they dislike have to say about that?"

I laughed, "I've had that discussion more than a few times. They say if no one cares, nothing will change. Someone has to do something about it."

"And?"

I laughed again, "I ask them if they're doing something about it."

"And how does that go over?"

I shook my head and smiled, "Not very well. I mean I do it all in a really nice way. I explain that I can see how passionate they are and how strongly they feel something should be done. *Then* I ask if they're doing something about it."

"And?"

I shook my head and smiled, "I've never had a person tell me they are. They talk a lot about how bad and unfair things are. But none of them try to change anything.

"So I explain that I decided to stop allowing things to annoy me unless I'm willing to invest my time to try and change them. It doesn't mean I like them. It just means I'm not going to give them my energy. I'm choosing to watch different channels."

"What do they say then?"

"Most of them get a little agitated and tell me, '*someone* needs to do something.' Then I smile, and let them know I think they are the perfect person to lead the effort. However, if they decide not to lead the effort, I suggest they let it go and focus on something else."

"How does *that* go over?"

"They usually get a little angry and say something mean. Which used to be uncomfortable for me. Except I had another 'aha!'."

ꕥ Chapter 38

Casey laughed, "And what was this other 'aha!'?"
"All anger is a manifestation of fear."
Casey nodded.

"I realized that when we're angry, if we ask ourselves 'Why?' it always comes down to a fear. It might require working down a few levels, but it's always there.

"For example, someone sees an article about a crooked politician who took money in exchange for approving a new building permit. As the person reads the article, they become incensed. When they talk about it, they become even more angry.

"They go on and on about crooked politicians and how corrupt everything has become.... Now on some level, it makes sense. The politician did do something wrong. So it isn't fair. However, the person's reaction is way out of proportion to their personal experience with what happened."

"Because they're afraid," Casey said.

"Exactly. Deep down, when they read that story about the crooked politician it ignites a fear fire inside of them. They get worried that if they ever need a building permit, it won't be available. The crooked politician will have given it to someone who paid them off. So then they'll be unable to build their dream house.

"Or worse yet, they won't be able to get a house. If they can't get a house they'll be homeless. Then they'll be hungry and without shelter, and won't be able to get a job. Their kids will be taken away from them. And...and...and...."

"They end up at fears which are a long way away from the original issue," Casey said.

I nodded, "That's what's so amazing. That's why this made my 'ahas!' book. I realized that anger is the result of these highly unlikely and pretty darn irrational fears. Mine included. So now, whenever I feel angry about something, I just ask myself—*what am I afraid of right now?* It's incredible how quickly I'll realize that my anger is driven by some non-related, irrational fear. So I can let it go."

Casey smiled, "Always?"

I smiled back, "It was kind of tough at the start. I mean I'm pretty laid back in general, but there were certain things which would really set me off. And I'd get angry. Because of my 'aha!' I knew the anger was really fear. I could rationalize it was getting me nowhere and didn't serve a positive purpose. But it was strange. Every once in a while, there was this part of me that wanted to..."

"Hang onto the anger?" Casey interjected.

I nodded, "Exactly! Like the anger was fuel for something."

I shrugged my shoulders and laughed.

"What is it?"

"Part of what really helped me came when I was sitting at this tiny little airport in Thailand. There was this old cartoon on television. Did you ever see one of those old cartoons like Tom and Jerry, where the little angel is on Tom's one shoulder and the little devil is on the other shoulder? And they're both trying to get him to do what they want?

"I realized, that's sort of like what hanging onto the anger felt like. The part of me which loves life and wants to grow and be in a state of flow, realized the real power was in letting go of the anger and irrational fear. That was the angel on my shoulder."

I smiled, "Only I think for me it's more like a fearless, little, world traveling guy who's very enlightened."

Casey laughed, "And who is on the other shoulder?"

"On the other shoulder is a very angry little caveman guy. Who is constantly living in fight or flight mode. Always afraid of what's around the corner and magnifying every fear a thousand times more than necessary."

Casey laughed again, "That's quite the visual. A battle between the enlightened little traveler and the angry little caveman."

"Only the battle never happened," I said. "That was the great 'aha!' within the 'aha!'. I thought the anger was fuel for the little caveman guy. But I realized he was just afraid. So the enlightened little traveler guy told the frightened little caveman guy it would all be OK. And over time they became friends and traveled the world together. Which is what the little caveman guy really wanted to do in the first place, but was too afraid to try."

Casey was laughing so hard I thought she would fall off her surfboard. "You really thought through all of this?" she asked.

I laughed too, "Sometimes you have to be a little crazy to get you over the crazy. And hanging onto that irrational kind of anger was definitely crazy."

"So this is how you dealt with the angry people who were glued to the three television channels they didn't like, huh?" Casey asked. "You saw their anger was really fear?"

I nodded, "That's it. I was able to look at them completely differently. I saw that more than anything else, they were afraid. So I tried to be like my little, friendly, enlightened traveler guy and let them know it would be OK. They weren't going to become homeless, and no one was going to take their children away.... It would all be OK."

"How did that go over?"

I shrugged and smiled, "I think most of the time they think I'm crazy. But I'm OK with that. I realized it comes down to a pretty basic decision. If you're so invested in something that you want to change it—then change it. That's awesome. For some people, that becomes their PFE and gives them a reason to get up every day."

I paused, "But if the truth is you aren't that invested in it, then you might as well focus your time and energy on a channel that does more for you than make you upset."

"A coward dies a thousand deaths, but a brave man only once," Casey said.

I looked at her confused.

"That was my reaction to that expression for the longest time," she said. "I'd heard it since I was a kid, but it never made sense. Then one day I was speaking with a customer at the café and it hit me. He was talking about a news story which bothered him greatly. About how people were abusing the health care system to get free treatment.

"Like what you were explaining, it was something so unrelated to his everyday life, but he was letting it make him really upset. His underlying fear was dominating him. And the more he thought about and talked about the news story, the angrier he became."

"He was dying a thousand deaths?" I asked.

She nodded, "Exactly. The coward lives in perpetual fear of all the things which might go wrong. In his mind, through his thoughts, he dies a thousand deaths. But the brave man realizes the pointlessness of allowing his mind to spiral out of control like that. He lives the life he wants to live."

She smiled, "We all die at some point. It's going to happen. But the brave person only goes through it once."

⌘ Chapter 39

Casey, Mike, Emma, Jessica and I surfed for hours. When we got tired we'd go back to the beach and rest or have a snack. Then it would be right back out into the water. It's incredible how easy it is to spend time doing what makes you happy. The day flew by.

As late afternoon settled in, the sun began to sink lower in the horizon. As it did, the sky took on a beautiful pink glow. The rays from the setting sun were reflecting back against clouds which were shaped like wispy feathers. It was perfection, spread as far across the horizon as you could see in either direction.

We had all paddled out just beyond the break and were watching the sun sink lower and lower.

"I can't believe I've been missing this," Jessica said. "I've gotten so busy being busy I never watch the sunset anymore."

"It's even better on a surfboard, isn't it?" Mike replied.

Jessica nodded and smiled, "Yes it is."

We were all silent for a while. The waves lapping against the edges of our boards, a soft warm breeze filling the air, the incredible sunset.... Perfection.

Jessica broke the silence with an excited cry. "A sea turtle!" she exclaimed. "Look, a sea turtle!"

Instinctively I glanced at Casey. When I'd visited the café previously, she had told me a story about a green sea turtle. The essence of the story was that if we aren't careful, we spend our time and energy going full out on the things which don't even matter to us that much. Then when opportunities come our way to do what we really want, we don't have time or energy for them.

If we aren't careful, we end up with a collection of life experiences far different than the life we truly want to live. All of this had been illustrated to Casey by watching the way a green sea turtle interacted with its surroundings.

That story had changed my life. It had crossed my mind almost every day since my night in the café. Now here we were and here was a green sea turtle right next to us! Perfection had just gotten even more perfect. I glanced at the turtle, then glanced at Casey again. She was looking at me and winked. Then nodded toward Jessica and the turtle.

I looked. The turtle had surfaced right next to Jessica's surfboard.

"That's Honu Honu," Emma said excitedly.

"Honu Honu?" Jessica asked.

"Honu means turtle in Hawaiian," Mike replied.

"See how he has a little bit of a hump on his shell?" Emma asked. "We see him out here every once in a while. I named him Honu Honu."

"Amazing," Jessica said. The turtle was just a few feet from her and she couldn't take her eyes off it.

"Casey has a really good story to share with you later about a green sea turtle," I said to Jessica.

"Really?" she replied and looked at Casey.

Casey smiled, "Sure," she said. "When we're back at the beach."

We watched Honu Honu for a while. He effortlessly made his way through the water. Always gliding along when the waves were with him and patiently waiting when the flow was against him.

"Ebb and flow," I said softly to myself.

Emma had heard it. She turned and looked at me, "What does that mean?"

"The movement of the water," I explained. "At times the current is pushing you, guiding you forward. That's flow. Practically effortless. Then at times, the current is going the other way. It's dragging you away from where you want to go."

"Like when you're done with surfing and trying to get back up on the beach," Emma said. "A wave will push you closer, and then after it hits the beach, it goes out and the current takes you back."

"Exactly."

"Why did you say it out loud?"

I nodded and smiled, "It's something I sometimes say to remind myself to take it easy. Just like the waves on the beach, I find life is a lot of ebb and flow."

I glanced at Jessica and then looked out at the sunset, "When you're in the ebb it feels like everything is going wrong. You feel like you're being dragged farther and farther from where you want to go. But there's always flow. Always. Sometimes that's easier to remember than other times."

I looked at Emma and laughed, "So I've taught myself that when I feel like I'm in the middle of *a lot* of ebbing..."

"The flow is coming," Jessica said quietly.

I looked at her and nodded, "Exactly. Ebb and flow. Ebb and flow. Just saying it calms me down. It reminds me the flow is coming."

↷ Chapter 40

The sun had almost sunk below the horizon.

"Time to start heading back, Coconut."

Emma turned to Mike, "Two more rides. Can we do two more rides?"

Mike smiled, "Two more." He glanced out at the waves, "Here comes the first one now."

A large wave was building. Mike and Emma both turned their boards and started to paddle.

Emma turned her head and looked back at us, "Are you coming?" she yelled.

"Next one," Casey yelled back.

The wave passed beneath us and I could hear the excited yells from Emma and Mike as they caught the wave and stood up on their boards.

"Ready?" Casey asked. Another large wave was building and coming toward us.

"All yours," I replied. "I'm going to catch a little smaller one."

"Me too," Jessica said.

"See you on the beach," Casey replied. She began to paddle. The wave came underneath us and a few moments later we saw Casey up on her board, surfing toward the shore.

Jessica turned and looked back out at the ocean. "It's been a great day," she said. "Thank you for convincing me to stay this morning."

I nodded, "My pleasure."

We both watched the ocean for a few moments.

"You know, there was a time when I was willing to give up most of my life because I didn't like it very much," I finally said.

"What do you mean?"

"I used to sit at work on Monday mornings and wish I could fast forward the clock to quitting time on Friday. I was willing to give up five days of my life each week, just to get to the days I did like."

I spread out my arms, "That's hard to imagine when you realize that *this* is what you can do with each day."

"The more you play in your playground, the less willing you are to be outside of it," Jessica said. She smiled, "Sorry. I just realized something for my own 'ahas!' book."

"Which is?"

"If I went to the beach once a week, I'd remember I love it so much. Then I'd arrange my life to go. But when I haven't been there for six months, I don't realize what I'm missing. So I allow myself to fill my time with things I really don't love as much."

She looked at me, "That's probably what happens when you travel, isn't it? You remember you love it so much that the energy carries you through your year of work until you go travel again."

I nodded, "It does. I supplement it too. When I come back from a trip, I print out a couple hundred pictures which remind me of the best parts of my adventures. They sell this little sticky type material you put right on the back of the picture and then put the picture right on the wall.

"I use it to put the pictures all over my place. So whether I'm brushing my teeth, stretching, having breakfast...I'm surrounded by that energy."

I laughed, "And of course I use my weekends to do little side trips too. No point in waiting the entire year to have some adventures."

"I want your life," she said and smiled.

"Do it," I replied. "Right now there are thousands of people living any and every life you might want to live. Why not be one of them?"

"I never thought of it like that."

"Someone's in Africa right now watching elephants. Another person is starting their own business, or going back to school, or choosing to spend more time with their kids.... It could be you."

"It *could* be me," she replied.

"The last time I visited the café, Casey shook me up with a little math," I said.

Jessica laughed, "Really?"

"Really. She showed me that spending just twenty minutes a day on little things I didn't really care about, like junk email, would end up costing me a year of my life. That inspired me. So let me see if I can inspire you with a little math I think about all the time.

"Most people get caught up in a trap. They think the goal of life is to make money, save money, and then live the life you want when you retire at sixty-five. The average life expectancy is about seventy-nine. So that means if you buy into that plan, you get about fourteen years of the really good stuff.

"Only what I've seen is that those years aren't all *golden*. People get sick, they have a tougher time getting around, some of their friends pass away.... Yes you can still live an incredibly active and fulfilling life after sixty-five. But the reality isn't always the happy, smiling, care free faces you see in the commercials. Age catches up to you."

"So do it now," Jessica said.

I nodded, "No one can ever take today away from you. This great day of surfing and fun and conversations.... The sunset and seeing the green sea turtle.... It's yours forever. You've put it in the bank. It doesn't matter what happens after you turn sixty-five.

"For me, I realized the system is backwards. Most people get really caught up in the fear they won't have enough in the future. So they kill themselves trying to be successful at jobs they don't like, forgo vacations with the people they love, give up their weekends.... And for what? The hope that they can cash in their points down the line?

"Well, let's turn the points into days. Imagine it all worked out to plan. At sixty-five they quit it all and start doing what they love. Those five days a week are now theirs. So they get five days times fifty two weeks, times fourteen years, which equals..."

"I got it," Jessica said.

She splashed some water on her surfboard and did the math in the droplets. "Three thousand, six hundred and forty," she said. "That sounds like a lot."

"It won't in a minute," I said and smiled.

"How many do you get if you choose a job where you get paid to do what you love?"

"Like surf," she said and smiled.

"Right now, somewhere around the world, there *are* people getting paid to surf," I said. "And there are tens of thousands of people who get paid to be around surfing. Everything you can imagine—accounting, graphic design, photography, product development, event promotion, marketing, and thousands more."

"It could be me," Jessica said.

"You, me, and anybody else who wants to," I said. "And how many days do they get?"

Jessica splashed some more droplets on her board. "Let's see, age twenty-two to age sixty-five is..."

"Actually it's twenty-two to seventy-nine," I said. "Those people are doing very well in those jobs. They get credit for those retirement years too."

Jessica redid the math. "Fourteen thousand eight hundred and twenty!"

"Four times as much," I said. "And you don't have to wait until the end to start enjoying it."

"So how come you don't do that?" Jessica asked. "You work for a year and then take a year off."

I nodded, "It's been a process for me. First it was letting go and taking a year off. Now it's the year at work, year off method." I smiled, "I've gotten a little lazy in looking for the perfect match. Where I would take every other year off to travel, and also log great minutes during the years I work. Being back here has inspired me, though. It's time to find that next level. I know its out there."

Jessica smiled, "Someone's doing it. It could be you."

I laughed, "It could be me."

໒ Chapter 41

"That was awesome!" Emma said. "Did you see us catch that last one?"

She and Mike had surfed their wave and then paddled back out for one more run.

"Jessica, do you want to ride next to me for your last one?" Emma asked. "We can take a smaller wave if you want."

Jessica smiled, "OK coach. You tell me when to get ready."

Mike patted Emma's surfboard, "Coconut, what do you think about having a little four person luau tonight after surfing? We can build a fire on the beach and eat down there."

"Yes, yes yes!" Emma replied and wiggled on her surfboard. "Can I invite Sophia and Tutu?"

Mike smiled, "Perfect. We'll make it a six person luau."

"You're going to love it, Jessica," Emma said. "It's *really* fun. We cook, and look at the stars, and dance!"

Jessica hesitated.

"You don't have to," Mike said.

She smiled, "No...I...I want to." She looked at me, "Someone's having fun at a luau tonight, right? Might as well be me."

I smiled, "Exactly. Might as well be you."

"Time to turn," Emma said. She patted Jessica's board.

Jessica glanced at the approaching wave, "Got it, coach."

Emma and Jessica turned their boards and started paddling.

"See you at the beach, Dad," Emma called back over her shoulder.

"OK," Mike called back. "Tell Casey about the luau."

The wave washed underneath us. We heard Emma and Jessica laughing as they stood up on their boards and started surfing toward the beach.

"How did you do it, Mike?" I asked. "She's a really special kid."

He smiled, "Thanks. It's been a great experience. Like I mentioned earlier, it's not everyone's path. For some people, there are other adventures which are more in line with their PFE. For me though, this has been a great adventure."

"Seeing how much fun you have with her, it seems hard to believe it *isn't* in line with everyone's adventures," I replied.

Mike laughed, "Maybe that's because you're getting the sense it's part of *yours.*"

I smiled, "I never really thought so. But the last few years I've started to wonder. Watching you and Emma...I guess I wonder even more. Is it as fun as it looks?"

Mike nodded, "Like most things in life, John, it's as fun as you allow it to be. Before I became a Dad, I made some conscious choices about the type of parent I wanted to be. Those have guided me well."

"Such as?"

"Well, the first one was realizing that when they arrive, babies already have their own spirit. As much as it's tempting to try to take ownership of Emma, the truth is, she's her own person. She has her own energy and her own path.

"She's mine in that biologically I'm her Dad and she's my daughter. At the same time, from the very first moment I looked at her and held her, I knew she was so much more than that. She was her own spirit. Arriving here with her own adventure ahead."

He shrugged, "I'm not sure if that makes sense to you. It's probably not something that would have made sense to me until I experienced it. I see it this way. She's my child and I would give my life for her in a second if need be. At the same time, I don't own her. I just get the great gift of being one of the people who gets to take care of her and be there for her."

"And teach her?" I asked.

"Sometimes," Mike replied. "All of us have something to share, so yes, sometimes part of my role is the teacher." He smiled, "And just as often, if not more often, she returns the gift and teaches me."

ᎧᏬ **Chapter 42**

"Really?" I said. "I never thought of it like that."

"It's there if you allow it to be," he replied. "It requires letting go of a lot. There's this ego, cultural, societal thing which tries to convince you that as the parent you know so much more than the child. Think of some of the expressions that still exist in our society."

"Children should be seen not heard," I said instinctively.

Mike nodded, "That's a perfect example. The implication is that the child's opinions or thoughts aren't as important as the adult's. But it's totally not true. If you allow yourself to interact from a person to person basis.

Or even better, a soul to soul basis, there's so much to share and learn."

He smiled, "When Emma was five, I took her to Africa. She is the type of personality where she likes to have her expectations set. If we're on the beach and I tell her we have to leave immediately, it's not a good experience. She feels the stress of that moment and responds accordingly. However, if I let her know we'll be leaving in five minutes, she'll pick up her beach toys on her own and be ready to go."

"I can relate to that," I said. "I like having my expectations set too."

"I do as well," Mike replied. "Which is maybe where she gets it from. But I don't think so. I think she arrived with that as part of her personality. She senses the energy and she doesn't like the energy of stress.

"Anyway," Mike continued, "since I knew she liked to have her expectations set, I let her know ahead of time that in order for us to go to Africa, she would need to get some shots. Well, at the start, it seemed like this time the approach completely backfired. She doesn't like shots, so she said she didn't want to go to Africa."

"What happened?"

He smiled, "It set the stage for both of us to teach each other. When she said she didn't want to go, there was a part of me that for just a flash of an instant, got angry inside."

"You?" I asked surprised.

"Those old patterns are in a lot of us," Mike replied. "It's just a matter of recognizing them for what they are. Not the truth, not the way things should go. Just an old pattern we experienced in our youth or that got lodged in our unconscious because we saw it playing out somewhere."

"When you felt that flash of anger, what were you afraid of?" I asked Mike.

"Excellent observation," he replied and smiled. "A realization captured in your book of 'ahas!' I bet. You're right. All anger is a manifestation of fear. My momentary flash of anger was the fear we wouldn't get to go to Africa."

"What did you do?"

"Well, those are the moments in life where you have a decision to make. I can take on the dominant parent role and give her a lecture. I can lash out without thinking and bring my fear to life...."

Mike changed the tone of his voice as if he were angry—"Do you know how lucky you are to travel to Africa? How many kids your age get to go and see the animals? And all you're doing is complaining! That's it! We're not going to Africa! And you're never watching your favorite animal shows on TV again...."

"That's painful to hear even though I know you're pretending," I said.

He nodded, "I know. And when I made those decisions about the kind of parent I wanted to be, one of them was that I wouldn't be *that* kind of parent."

"So what did you do instead?"

"When Emma said she didn't want to go, I picked her up, put her in my lap and wrapped my arms around her. In a quiet, calm voice I told her I understood. I didn't like shots either. Then I explained that as an adventurer, which she is, you can't let the small things keep you from the big things.

"Getting a shot isn't fun. It also doesn't take long. In five minutes, you're done. Yes your arm hurts a little bit." He smiled, "Although even that can be lessened if you go out for ice-cream to celebrate you are 'Africa Ready'.

"The point is, getting a shot is a small thing compared to going to Africa and being right there with the animals."

"So you shared that with her?"

"I did. Then I asked her what she thought."

"And she said she'd do it?" I asked.

He nodded. "And by the way," he said. "That same decision is in front of us, in all our interactions. Whether it's parent and child, two adults, a boss and an employee.... Moment by moment, every day, we can choose the high road where we take time to connect to the other person and see things from their perspective. Or, we let fear turn to anger, and try to bulldoze our way to what we want."

"So you went to Africa," I said.

"And when we were there, Emma taught the exact same lesson back to me," Mike replied.

I laughed, "Really?"

He nodded, "Uh huh. We had an incredible time there. On one day though, I was tired from a tough day of driving. We had been on the road for about four weeks and that particular day had been five hours on tough, dangerous, very bumpy roads. When we finally arrived at this remote campsite we were driving to, it was more remote than I'd expected. There was almost nothing there.

"It was getting dark and I was worried about getting everything up before night fell. Plus, I'd expected a place to buy food and there wasn't one. So even though we carried our own supplies, some part of me was concerned about what I'd get Emma to eat.

"Then, when I was trying to put up our tent, I couldn't get the anchor rods to align right. Three times in a row, the tent collapsed. And I felt overwhelmed. Just completely overwhelmed by the day, the moment.... As I was standing there, taking a few deep breaths and trying to put it in perspective, Emma came up and wrapped her arms around my legs.

"She could tell I was frustrated and asked me if I was OK. I told her I was just frustrated with the tent."

"Well Dad," she said in her enthusiastic, little voice, "you can't let the small things keep you from the big things. I mean putting up the tent is a small thing, but being here in Africa is a big thing. We'll get the tent up. But we should be grateful we're all the way here in Africa and get to see the animals and stuff. I mean not many people get to do that and we're right here and everything."

Mike laughed and shook his head, "It wasn't just what she said, which was perfect. It was the way she said it. It was so matter of fact, and loving, and enthusiastic, and full of wisdom. And yet at the same time, said with the words of a five year old. I picked her up and spun her around a dozen times. And then a dozen times more when she kept saying 'again, again.'"

"And you got the tent up?" I said and smiled.

"Got the tent up, got food, slept well, and continued on with the adventure the next day," Mike replied.

"It's hard to imagine you being frustrated or angry," I said. "You always seem so calm to me. Like nothing gets to you."

He smiled, "I believe that's me at my best. My most authentic. Which is my intention for every moment. And I do my utmost to allow my energy to live in that state as often as possible."

He shrugged, "But I have my times when I'm not at my best. I'm not happy about that. And I make a conscious effort to shorten my time in that energy."

"How do you do that?"

"By being the observer to the moment, not just the participant in the moment."

ᕫ Chapter 43

Emma and Jessica made their way up the beach toward the café. They were carrying their surfboards. The sun had completely sunk below the horizon. The pink glow on the clouds was starting to fade away.

Jessica turned and looked out at the ocean, "Thank you Emma," she said and smiled. "Today was one of the best days of my life."

"Great! Maybe you should come back tomorrow and we can do it again."

Jessica laughed. It seemed so obvious.

"Do the things you like to do, and don't do the things you don't like to do," Emma said. "That's what my Dad taught me and it's totally true. Since you liked surfing, do it again."

"Good advice, coach," Jessica replied. She looked out at the beautiful sky and the ocean. "Any final pieces of surfing wisdom for me?"

Emma thought for a minute. "Well, since you're new to surfing, maybe remember this one. My Dad taught it to me when I was little and I always remember it."

Jessica laughed to herself. It was so funny to hear a seven year old describe a time when they were *little*.

"I'm ready," Jessica said.

"OK. It's three words. Each letter of the words stands for something. One of the words isn't even grammatically correct, but that's OK. It's just to help you remember. The words are—*I a sage*."

"I a sage?"

"Uh huh. I didn't know what that meant when my Dad first told it to me. But he explained a sage is a wise person. So then it kind of made sense, because if you remember these things, they help you a lot. So then you're pretty wise."

Jessica smiled, "And what does '*I a sage*,' stand for?"

"The 'I' is for intuition. Great surfers are really intuitive about picking their waves and the way they ride them. They sort of flow with the waves instead of being separate from them. You see some people who are new and they don't use their intuition at all. They are so worried about every step, and what to do next, and they fall *a lot!*"

Jessica laughed, "Got it. That's the I."

"The 'a' stands for always another wave. My Dad explained that if you get mad because you missed a wave, then while you're sitting there being mad, you'll miss two more. If you miss a really good one, admire it for what it was and be happy you were there to see it. But don't spend all your time regretting you missed it. There's always another one."

"Always another wave," got that one too.

"'S' is for start small and work your way up."

"Like what you did with me today," Jessica said.

"Uh huh. My Dad started me in the white water and for a long time I just did that. Then it got a little boring and I wanted to try the waves. So he started me on the small waves. Then those got a little boring and now I surf the bigger ones. Someday I want to do the pipeline...but not yet."

Jessica nodded, "The pipeline looks amazing, doesn't it? I can't even imagine what it must be like to be in that little circular space as the wave is crashing right over you. And to somehow have so much confidence and control you can stay on your feet and ride right through to freedom."

Emma nodded, "It looks really awesome. That's why I want to surf it. I just want to work up to it. I've met some adults who tried it too early and crashed pretty bad. Now they won't even try it again. And they're not even that old!"

Jessica smiled.

"The other 'a' is for ask. My friend Sophia and I do this all the time. We'll watch for the best surfers and then ask them for advice."

"And do they help you?"

"Well, not always. Some of them don't. But most of them are really nice." She shrugged, "Can't let the small things keep you from the big things. Someone not being nice is a small thing. It felt kind of bad at first, but now we just go right on to the next person and ask them. Riding great waves is a big thing. We don't want to miss out on that just because someone wasn't nice."

"Got it. What's the 'g' for?"

"Can we save the 'g' for last, because that's my favorite?"

Jessica smiled, "OK. We'll save that one for last. What's the 'e' for?"

"Every great surfer had a day when they didn't know how to stand on a board. I mean it's *really* hard to believe when you see the surfers who are so good. But it's true. When they started they didn't even know how to stand up. So if they can learn to surf so good, so can I."

Jessica nodded. It reminded her of John's comment about becoming an expert. "OK, coach. What's your favorite?"

Emma smiled and said at the top of her lungs, "'G'. The only way to really screw up a day of surfing is to *not* GO! So GO!" Then she did a little happy dance.

Jessica laughed.

"You can do the happy dance if you want to," Emma said. "This is called the go surfing shuffle. I made it up. You don't have to get all the steps right, you can just do your best."

Jessica lifted her feet. She felt awkward compared to the free spirited, effortless movements Emma made. "Just go," she thought to herself. "Just go!" And for the next few minutes, she allowed herself to effortlessly and without a moment of self-evaluation, dance the go surfing shuffle with Emma.

Chapter 44

The light was quickly fading from the sky. It would be dark soon.

Mike glanced out at the disappearing horizon, "About time to head in," he said.

I knew he was right. I also had a deep sense there was something really important in his comment. About being an observer to the moment, not just a participant in the moment.

"How about a quick example of being the observer?" I asked. "Then we'll catch the next wave in. Something tells me you have a really good story about that."

Mike splashed some water on his board and smiled, "OK," he said. "One quick story. Not one of my finer moments, but certainly one for my own personal book of 'ahas!'.

"While Emma and I were traveling, we had a stretch in Australia where we rented a camper-van. Which is basically a van which you can sleep in at night. It was an experiment. We'd done a lot of camping, which had gone great. So we thought we'd try this. It seemed like a fun idea, and I'm sure for some people it works out well...."

"But not for the two of you," I said.

He shook his head, "Not for us. It was just too tough to sleep. I don't know exactly why, but it was so small and the logistics of it just weren't a good fit. And the worst part was that for some reason, we'd both wake up in the middle of the night and have to go to the bathroom."

"Never a good thing," I said.

"Especially not when it means leaving the camper-van and walking over to the bathroom areas in the middle of the night," Mike said. "We're pretty good about roughing it in lots of ways, but for some reason this just wasn't a good fit."

"So what happened?"

"Emma had been such a trooper. Never complaining. Always a positive attitude. After about three weeks of waking up in the middle of the night and both of us having to walk to the bathroom though, she had a meltdown. She woke at two in the morning and no matter how much I told her it was OK, she just kept crying. And she was loud. *Really* loud.

"So I searched around our tiny, cramped quarters and finally found her shoes and put them on. Then, with her still crying, I frantically searched for my own shoes and put them on. Finally, I picked her up and carried her the five minutes to the bathroom area. The whole time she's crying at the top of her lungs."

He shook his head, "These areas where you park your campervan for the night are full of other people doing the same thing. And it's pretty annoying when you get woken up in the middle of the night because someone else is being really loud.

"So I was very aware that at two in the morning and the volume Emma was crying, we were going to wake *everyone* up."

I nodded, "What happened?"

"We get to the bathroom and I'm thinking she'll calm down, but she doesn't. It's so completely out of character for her, but she's just complaining and crying uncontrollably."

Mike shook his head, "I never like to do it, because I think it's a lousy precedent to set. But I was so concerned about everyone else at the campground, that I tried to get her to stop crying by threatening to take away things she liked. My voice got very quiet, and very direct. I told her if she didn't stop, she wouldn't be able to use her favorite toy the next day."

"Did it work?" I asked.

"Not at all. She wailed even louder." Mike shrugged, "So I told her if she didn't stop, we wouldn't go to the animal sanctuary the next day. Which was something she'd been looking forward to for a week."

"And?"

"That just made her cry even more."

Mike splashed some water on his board. He shook his head, "It was me at my worst. That's not who I am as a person, and definitely not the type of Dad I am."

"What happened next?" I asked.

"I saw her."

I gave him a confused look, "What do you mean?"

"It was powerful, and surreal, and a gift from somewhere…. When we'd gotten to the bathroom, I'd put her up on the toilet. She was so tired, I was afraid she would fall off, so I was kneeling in front of her and holding her.

"That's where we were when I told her about taking away the trip to the animal sanctuary. Only something happened as I was telling her. In addition to saying those words, I also heard them. I heard them like someone else was saying them. I was the observer to the scene even though I was part of the scene."

Mike shook his head a little, "And in that role of the observer..." He paused. I saw how real and emotional the memory was. He started to speak again, but choked up and had to wait for a moment.

Eventually, he looked at me and smiled through the emotion, "In that role of the observer, I saw this tiny little human. Who was *so* tired, and *so* brave, and always had such a great attitude. And I saw her soul and her spirit and I felt the pain she was in. I felt it at a place in my own heart I didn't even know I had. My heart welled up so much I thought it would burst."

I nodded, "What did you do?"

"I wiped the tears from her little cheeks, and put her face against my shoulder and told her it was alright. That everything was alright. I told her Daddy was here, and everything was alright. And in my mind, I realized what a fool I'd been. I was so concerned about everyone else in the campground, I was forgetting the person who mattered most to me in the world.

"She put her arms around my neck and I pulled her little pajamas up. Then I held her to my chest with every ounce of compassion I had in me. I whispered in her ear that I loved her and I was so happy she was my daughter."

Mike wiped a tear from the corner of his eye, "I will never forget that experience," he said. "I thought I was a good father up to then. That night instilled in me a deep drive to always be better. To always challenge myself to raise my own level of connectedness with what I am truly capable of."

"To be the participant *and* the observer for your own life," I added.

He nodded, "That's exactly it. Am I willing to think for just a microsecond before I speak? To see what the impact will be, especially in times of frustration or anger? Can I glance at a moment and see it all as it's unfolding? Then adjust my part in it, because I have the presence to become the observer as well as the participant?"

He smiled, "It's an incredible gift to give yourself. It's the realization you are not your physical body. You are your spirit, which just happens to be residing in your physical body right now. With that realization, so much of the fear, anger, worry and frustrations in life lift away. Which is what Emma reminded me of that night at the campground."

ಌ Chapter 45

Mike and I picked a wave and rode it in for the last ride of the night. When we arrived on the beach, Emma came racing down the trail to greet us. At full speed, she ran to Mike and with her arms wide open, wrapped herself around his legs. "Hi, Daddy."

He put down his board, picked her up and gave her a kiss on the cheek. Then he lifted her over his back, held onto her ankles and spun around. "Where's Emma?" he said, as if he didn't know she was hanging behind him. "Seriously, John, have you seen her? She was just here a minute ago. Emma! Emma!" he pretended to call.

Emma was a fit of giggles, "I'm right behind you," she said through her laughing.

Mike pulled her back up over his shoulder so she was in front of him again, "Oh, there you are. I couldn't find you for a minute."

Emma laughed and put her hands on his face, "We have a fire going, and Sophia and Tutu will be here soon. It's time for the luau."

She squirmed to the ground and ran back toward the café.

"Looks like it's time for the luau," Mike said and smiled.

He picked up his board and we both continued on toward the café. As we did, I couldn't help but think how his choices in the campground, his choices each time I'd seen him interact with Emma, led to moments like I'd just witnessed.

∞ Chapter 46

Mike and I walked in silence for a few moments.

"In addition to the campground experience you told me about," I said, "what's the best decision you've made as a dad?"

Mike paused and thought for a moment, "The day she was born I made the decision I would never yell at Emma."

"Really?" I replied. I'd seen a lot of parents over the years and yelling seemed like a standard part of parenting.

"That's what you notice most when you don't have kids of your own," he said.

It only threw me a tiny bit that he'd read my mind.

"And there are a lot of people who choose to be like that," he added.

"You chose differently?"

He nodded, "I did. I was right there when Emma arrived. I held her, cleaned her, stroked her tiny little head." He smiled, "She was the size of a coconut. So little, so delicate, and yet so present somehow. Her eyes were open right away and she looked at me with this calm presence. Like she understood the secrets of the universe. I decided in that moment, I would never raise my voice to her, never yell at her."

"And?"

"She's seven now. I never have, and I never will."

"How do you handle it when she does something wrong?" The idea of not yelling at your kids seemed so foreign to me. I had a hard time envisioning a life without it.

"We accept behavior from ourselves based on how we define ourselves. On the day she was born, I defined myself as a father who would never yell. So if I did yell, it would be out of character, out of synch with who I am."

I gave Mike a confused look.

"Think of it this way," he said. "If you defined yourself as an adventurer, would it seem normal or abnormal to never leave your house?"

I smiled, "Abnormal."

"Exactly. If someone tried to force you to stay in your home, it wouldn't feel right. Not emotionally, not physically, not intellectually.... You defined yourself as an adventurer, which means you go on adventures. To always stay at home then would be unacceptable. You would refuse to act that way."

"I think I get it," I replied. "Since you defined yourself as a father who doesn't yell, then if you were to yell, it wouldn't feel right. Not emotionally, physically, or intellectually."

He nodded, "Exactly." Then he smiled, "And the universe likes to test you on your conviction to these things."

I smiled back, "In what way?"

"Like on a day when you're exhausted from a dozen unexpected events. And you feel the stress from those unexpected events. And it's late, and you're thinking about all you still have to get done that night, and all that needs to be done to make it through the day tomorrow.... And that's the time when your child wants to goof around instead of brushing their teeth."

"And you feel like yelling?"

"You do. You feel the stress and the tension. And there's this part of you which knows a quick way out. Yell as loud as you can and intimidate everyone around you into doing what you want done."

"But you don't do it."

He shook his head, "Not if you're true to who you say you are. See, John, at the same time the stress is inside of you, if you're willing to step outside the experience, like we talked about earlier, it changes everything."

"In what way?"

"Well, for starters, you realize your stress and frustration has nothing to do with whether or not someone is brushing their teeth. You're about to take out your anger on someone who didn't cause it. And that's not fair. If you're determined to get mad at someone, get mad at who's making you mad. Direct your anger at those who are making you angry.

"Don't direct it at those who just happen to be around, or those you know you're more powerful than." He paused for a moment, "And most especially, don't direct it at someone just because you know they'll forgive you."

I nodded. That was powerful. How often I'd seen someone lash out at a family member. When in reality, the family member had nothing to do with what the person was angry about.

"There's another piece too," Mike continued. "When you have defined yourself as someone who doesn't yell, when the urge to yell starts building inside of you, it feels wrong."

"Like an adventurer staying inside the house," I added.

"Exactly. In this case, you may feel an initial urge to yell. But when you do, you'll feel an even more powerful force which says, 'That's not who you are. You have chosen to be a father who *doesn't* yell.'

"Therefore it would feel far more uncomfortable to yell. So you don't. That remembrance, that realization, calms you down. It helps you put things in perspective. It enables you to be the authentic you that you have chosen to be, instead of allowing some cultural or behavioral conditioning to drive your actions.

"It gives you the awareness to step outside of the situation. To be the observer, even for just a few seconds.

In those seconds, you are so much more clear about what your authentic response is. Then you act in spirit with that."

I shook my head a little, "It might be because it's the first time I'm hearing all this, Mike, but it sounds complex."

He nodded, "I understand. If you think about it in its most basic elements though, it's really pretty simple. First you define who you are. Then you allow yourself to step outside of the moment at times. View life from the perspective of both the participant and the observer. That only takes a second. Maybe even less. Then you act based on those things."

"And it works?"

He laughed, "Even on the toughest days."

Mike turned to me, "I'll give you one more thought to muse on, John. Would you invite someone to your house and then yell at them because you're angry at someone else?"

I laughed, "That would probably be the last time they ever came over."

"Indeed. Yet people do that all the time. They invite those they love into their lives, which is way more significant than just inviting them into their house. Then they use them as an outlet to vent their anger."

I shook my head, "I never thought about it like that. But you're right. I've seen people talking to their spouse, or partner, or kids, in ways they would never talk to a guest in their house. Or even to their best friend."

We were almost to the campfire. Mike stood up his board for a moment. He smiled, "When we recognize the insanity in our behavior, we have the choice to stop being insane. Some of the greatest gifts Emma has given me are the types of life lessons we've been talking about. Because they don't just apply to a parent and a child. They apply to all of our interactions."

He picked up his board again, "There's a fresh water hose and shower over there," he said and indicated toward a small grove of tropical trees. "Why don't we rinse everything quick and then join the luau."

I started walking with my board toward the rinsing area. "How right he is," I thought to myself. I'd been processing our conversations in the context of Mike and Emma—parent and child. Yet the lessons were applicable in so many ways beyond a parent and child too.

It was time to grab my 'ahas!' book. I wanted to remember these things.

෴ Chapter 47

"You guys made it."

Mike and I had washed off the boards and ourselves. Then he'd gone into the café to check on Emma and Casey. I'd wandered over to the beach fire.

Jessica was sitting in the sand, leaning against a large piece of volcanic rock. There were many big rocks, all arranged in a circle. In the middle of them, a small fire was crackling.

Jessica smiled, "We thought maybe you two decided to do a little night surfing."

I smiled back, "Next time. No, we were just having some great conversations and the time flew by."

Jessica nodded, "I know the feeling. That seems to be a regular experience at this place."

I sat down next to her, "You look happy. Content."

She nodded, "I don't know what it is exactly. I just feel lighter. I feel like..."

"Like the way life is supposed to feel?" I added.

She nodded, "Yeah. Like before today I was trapped in a box and didn't know how to get out. Now the box is gone, and I feel like it was never really there in the first place. I just thought it was there. I'd convinced myself it was real for so long, that it became real in my mind. But now it's gone."

She looked at me, "Does that make sense?"

I nodded, "I felt a lot like that the first time I visited the café. I hung out there all night. When I left in the morning, I had this sense of understanding." I shrugged, "I'm not even sure I knew what it was I understood, but things felt clearer. And like you said, lighter."

"Does it last?" she asked. "Part of me is almost a little afraid to keep feeling this way. It feels so right, that if it goes away...I know it will feel so awful."

I smiled, "The poet would say it is better to have felt and lost than never to have felt at all." I shook my head a little and laughed, "I'm not really a poet though. So here's my take. The first time I was here, Casey explained to me that this feeling, this sense of knowing, is like seeing a treasure map and knowing where the X is. Once you've seen it, you always know it's there."

"That's a good thing," Jessica said. "Right?"

I nodded, "It is...." Then I hesitated.

"What is it?" she asked.

"It *is* a good thing. It's a great thing actually," I added more emphatically. "With every 'aha!' you have, you see the way things really work. You start to understand life on a totally different level. And with each adventure you go on which is in line with your PFE and Big Five for Life, you experience living in a way you couldn't even imagine before."

I shrugged, "There will come a point when you have to *really* struggle to remember what it used to be like. When you felt like you were in the box. When you saw the world as a place of limitations versus a playground of infinite possibilities."

"That all sounds incredible," Jessica said. "So why the hesitation a minute ago?"

"Because once you arrive at that point, you won't accept a life inside the box."

"I don't want to accept a life inside the box. I want *this* feeling," she said emphatically.

I nodded and smiled, "I understand. It's important for you to understand something, though. Sometimes that comes with a price."

She looked at me quizzically, "What kind of price?"

I shrugged again, "I can only tell you my experience. I found that once I started to change, some of my friendships didn't make sense any more. Some of my family relationships too."

"Why?"

"Well, I learned some people liked me as the guy in the box. That's what they knew. That's who they felt comfortable being around. They wanted someone who saw the world like they did. When I stopped seeing it that way, they felt threatened."

"What happened?"

"At first they tried to put the box back around me. Little things. They'd complain about how unfair things were in the world, or what a jerk their boss was. Or engage me in a long discussion about some tragedy they saw on the news, or the gossip of the day about some celebrity."

"But that wasn't you anymore," Jessica said.

I shook my head, "No, it wasn't. I didn't want to be part of that energy. It was fine if they did. That was their choice and I wasn't going to judge them. I just didn't want to be."

"So what happened?"

"Over time, some of my old friendships faded away. Same with some of my family relationships. What I found though, is once I opened that space up, I now had room for new friendships, and new relationships. Ones that were more in line with who I had become and who I aspired to be in the future."

I shrugged, "I decided I would rather be me and be happy, than someone else's version of me and be stuck on OK."

Jessica nodded, "That seems like a good decision. You seem very comfortable being you. *This* you."

"I am. I'll tell you though, it doesn't always sit well with people."

"Really?"

"Sure. I live a pretty different lifestyle. I do what I want, when I want. I don't have a house or a car. Every other year I'm out traveling around somewhere. For many people, that's hard to figure out. It scares them."

"In what way?"

"Because it challenges their own belief system. Based on their view of the world, at my age I'm *supposed* to be putting a certain amount in a 401K retirement plan. I'm supposed to have *this* type of car, live in *that* type of neighborhood, do *these* types of activities, and be in *that* type of relationship.... So when I'm not, part of their mind starts to get confused. '*Maybe I don't need to be doing all that either*,' it thinks."

"Why am I here?" Jessica said thoughtfully.

I nodded. "I know. That question is clearly on the café menu for a reason. Because when you get right down to it, it doesn't matter what anyone else thinks you *should* be doing, or *need* to be doing. That's just a collective opinion based on what the majority of people *are* doing. Which more often than not is based on what an advertiser would *like them* to be doing."

I smiled, "It's like—'Oh, you're a woman between thirty and thirty-five? Most women between thirty and thirty-five have a job, a family, a three bedroom two bath house, and drive a SUV. So that's what you should have too.'"

"And so you start to live your life just like the script," Jessica said. "You end up living this pre-defined life. Whether you're twenty, fifty, eighty..."

"Unless..." I said and paused.

"Unless I ask myself—*Why am I here?*" Jessica said. "And then create a new script, *my* script. One that allows me to live the life I want. In the way I want."

I nodded, "That's what I've learned." Then I smiled at Jessica.

"What is it?"

I shrugged, "Sometimes I wonder if that right there is the whole point of life. It's just a giant game and the whole point is to see if you can remember to live the life *you* want to live. To realize you are actually in control of the game, instead of the game controlling you."

"To build your own playground," Jessica replied thoughtfully, "and play in it as much as you want."

◯◯ Chapter 48

"They're here! They're here!"

Emma ran out the back door of the café and onto the sand.

"Hi Sophia! Hi Tutu!" she said excitedly.

I turned to see who she was talking to.

A young girl and an older Hawaiian woman were getting hugs from Emma.

"That young girl is Sophia. She's Emma's friend," Jessica said. "I saw them playing together earlier today."

"Who is the other woman?"

"I'm not sure."

I stood up. Jessica did as well.

Emma led her friends over to the fire pit.

"John and Jessica, these are my friends. This is Sophia and her grandma. We call her grandma, Tutu. Because that's how you say grandma in Hawaiian."

I knelt down so I was eye level with Sophia and extended my hand, "Nice to meet you, Sophia."

She shook my hand, "Nice to meet you too," she said and gave me a shy smile.

I stood and switched places with Jessica. She had just greeted Tutu. Now it was my turn.

Tutu had a presence and sense about her which suggested she knew much about life. Her eyes sparkled and her energy was so apparent, it seemed you could reach out and touch it. Had it not been for the occasional streak of gray in her long, dark, hair, it would have been almost impossible to guess her age. Her youthful energy was that strong.

"Aloha, John," she said and gave me a warm hug.

"Aloha," I replied.

When we separated, I smiled at her. She reached up and touched the side of my face, "It is good to have you back at the café," she said and returned my smile.

I wasn't sure how she knew I'd been there before. Maybe Emma had told Sophia, and Sophia had told her. Or maybe she just knew. I sensed it was the latter.

Tutu was wearing a traditional Hawaiian dress and Sophia was tugging on it. Tutu reached down and touched her head. "What is it little one?" she asked in a soft voice.

"Can we give them their flowers now?" Sophia whispered.

Tutu smiled, "I think Mike and Casey will be out in just a moment. How about if we wait for them and then give everyone their flowers?"

Sophia's face was beaming and she nodded her little head up and down.

As if on cue, Mike and Casey came out of the café. Each was carrying a large tray of food. They walked over to us.

"Hello, Sophia. Hello, Tutu," Casey said when she got closer.

Casey put down her tray and hugged each of them. So did Mike.

"We've got *lots* of really good stuff to eat," Emma said.

I looked at the trays. It was a feast. Fresh pineapple and papaya, whole grilled fish, rice wrapped in banana leaves....

"Just the thing for some hungry surfers," Mike said and smiled.

"Jessica learned to surf today, Tutu," Emma said.

"Were you her teacher?" Tutu asked.

"Uh huh."

"Are you a surfer too?" Jessica asked Tutu.

"She's an awesome surfer," Emma interjected. "Tutu is the one who taught Sophia. It's in her blood. The Hawaiian people are the ones who invented surfing."

"Really?" Jessica asked surprised. "I thought it was a California thing."

Tutu wrapped her arms around Emma and kissed the top of her head. "It was invented here," she said. "A very long time ago. The Hawaiian people have always been deeply connected to the water." She smiled, "After all, we live on a small group of islands in the middle of a very large ocean."

"Tutu, can I give them out now?" Sophia whispered.

Tutu looked down at her and smiled, "Yes little one."

Sophia opened the large basket Tutu had carried over. She reached inside and pulled out a beautiful necklace made of real flowers. Then she walked over to Jessica. "Aloha, Jessica. This is for you. It's called a lei."

Jessica smiled and knelt in the sand so Sophia could reach her head. She bowed a little and Sophia gently placed the flowers around her neck.

"Thank you, Sophia," Jessica said softly and smiled.

"In Hawaiian culture, we express our connection to another soul by giving them a lei," Tutu explained. "It is a tradition that goes back over a thousand years. We use it to express love, gratitude, forgiveness, peace...." She smiled, "And as a celebration of the life spirit too."

One by one, Sophia gifted a lei to each of us.

They smelled incredible. The sweet fragrance of their flowers filled the air.

"Thank you, Sophia and Tutu for the beautiful lei," Mike said. "How about if we continue our celebration with some food. Is anyone hungry?"

"Me!" Emma yelled.

"Me too!" Sophia added.

"Well then I guess we'll start with you two," Mike replied and smiled.

౼ Chapter 49

The food was amazing. We ate until we couldn't take another bite. Then Casey grabbed some cushions from the café and we settled in around the fire. Except for Emma and Sophia. They were playing together, making sandcastles and decorating them with shells.

"Casey and Mike, that was incredible. Thank you," I said.

Casey lifted her glass, "Welcome back," she replied. "And thanks for your help in the kitchen this morning."

"Was that only this morning?" I asked. "It seems so long ago. This has been such an incredible day."

Jessica nodded, "It does seem hard to believe that was only this morning. It feels like a lifetime ago somehow."

Casey smiled, "The concept of a day takes on new meaning when you fill it with meaningful events, doesn't it?"

"It does," Jessica said thoughtfully. "It really does."

"So why don't we do that?" She added. She looked around at the group and laughed, "I guess more accurately, why don't *I* do that. It seems like each of you has figured that part of life out."

"John, what's your take on that?" Mike asked. "You're just coming back from another year of adventure filled days."

I thought for a moment. "Part of it for me was letting go of the never ending To Do list," I said.

"What do you mean?" Jessica asked.

"Before I came to the café the first time, I was living a very busy life. Only it was busy with activities which weren't what I really wanted to be doing. I just felt like if I could get through them all, then finally I'd be free. If I could just clear off all the items on my To Do list, then I could go live the life I wanted."

"How'd that work out for you?" Mike asked with a grin.

I smiled, "About as poorly as you can imagine. The list never got completed. No sooner had two things gotten done than two more were added. There seemed to be a never ending string of responsibilities."

"That's exactly how I feel most days," Jessica said. "I came here to this beautiful island but I never enjoy it. I keep thinking if I put in a little extra time at work, take some things home, come in on the weekend...that I'll eventually get caught up and be free. But it never happens."

"The universe is watching," Casey said quietly.

"You're right," Jessica said. "You're so right."

"The universe is watching?" I asked.

Jessica looked at Casey. "Go ahead," Casey said. "You know."

For the next few minutes, Jessica explained what that meant. And how she and Casey had discussed it earlier in the day.

When she finished, I nodded, "I've never thought of it in those terms, but I've found that to be exactly right. You get more of what you spend your time on. So the key is to put the important things into your life first. After that, if there's any room left, then add the rest."

Tutu laughed softly, "There is a beautiful illustration of that in Polynesian folklore," she said. "It is the story of the silly sailor and his outrigger canoe."

"Can we hear it?" Jessica said.

"Oh, can we do the dance?" Emma asked excitedly. "Yes, can we?" Sophia added.

"I didn't know the two of you were listening," Tutu said with a smile.

"We've been playing *and* listening," Sophia replied.

"Well, if you would like to do the dance, you'll need music," Tutu said and looked at Mike.

He smiled, "Be right back." He got up and jogged over to the café. A few minutes later he returned with a ukelele and three drums.

"These are pahu," he said and handed a drum to Jessica, Casey and me. "They're native Hawaiian drums."

I took mine and tapped it a few times.

Mike turned to Tutu, "Will you do us the honor of being the story teller?"

She smiled and nodded.

"Then I guess Sophia and I will dance, and you'll play ukelele," Mike said and pretended to hand the ukelele to Emma.

"No," she said and giggled. "*You* play ukelele and *I'll* dance with Emma."

Mike pretended to be surprised, "Oh! So that's what we're going to do. OK." He smiled and sat down on the sand.

"OK my dancers, come close," Tutu said. "Do you remember the movements?"

Both little girls nodded enthusiastically.

"Then it is time for the story of the silly sailor and his outrigger canoe."

෨ **Chapter 50**

Tutu turned to Jessica and I and smiled, "My new drummers, you have a very experienced drummer who will lead you. And a very experienced ukelele player too. They know this song very well. Simply follow their lead, and have fun."

I nodded. Jessica looked at me and smiled. Then she placed her hands above her drum.

Mike started softly playing the ukelele. When Casey joined in and started drumming quietly along with him, Jessica and I joined in too.

Tutu began slowly and rhythmically swaying to the sounds. Her hips moved in that soft, gentle way that so personifies the graceful art of Hawaiian dancing. The girls moved next to her and began swaying with her.

After a few moments, and in time with the music, Tutu began rhythmically telling the story.

"From the rivers to the oceans,
from the stars on to the sun,
we seek our new adventures,
finding laughter and some fun.

Explorers of it all,
adventures big and small,
step one for us to do,
is to fill our big canoe.

"That is the credo of the polynesian adventurer," Tutu said dramatically and raised her arms to the sky.

Casey began to beat crazily on her drum. Jessica and I joined in and did the same. The girls, who had been doing slow gestures in accompaniment to Tutu's words, now danced wildly, their arms also raised to the sky.

Tutu smiled and once again began slowly and rhythmically swaying her hips to the ukelele music. When our crazy drumming had calmed down, she extended her arm and swept it across her chest.

"Today we tell the story,
of the silly sailor who,
could never start his voyage,
for he could not pack his canoe.

On the beach were all his things,
to maybe take along his trip.
Not all of same importance,
and that would be his slip.

What mattered most he set aside,
those he would put in last.
His surfboard, spear, paddle and hat,
must-haves for his adventures vast.

Up and down the beach front,
gathered people from far and wide.
They all had their opinion,
on what he should put inside.

Take this, take this, take this again,
was the call from many who,
had never sailed the ocean,
never dipped in waters blue.

Take that, take that, take that again,
was the call from different ones,
who'd spent their lives just wishing,
for adventure and some fun.

The calls rang out, they kept it up,
for hours and more it seemed.
And the silly sailor did his best,
to hear every voice between.

He packed his canoe, he filled it up,
a hundred times and more.
But always at the very end,
his favorite things were still on shore.

Take this, take this, take this again,
called the people more and more.
Take that, take that, take that again,
their voices would all soar.

They go in last, he said steadfast,
of the things that mattered most.
So time went by and still he was,
stuck upon the sandy coast.

How do I do it, he thought to himself,
upset at what wouldn't go.
Yet he still refused, to put in first,
the things that mattered so.

Day after day, then weeks and more,
all passed, then he felt a drip.
The rainy season, upon him now,
would he ever take his trip?"

OOGA OOGA OOGA OOGA
OOGA OOGA OOGA OOGA

Mike had started chanting. Emma and Sophia had joined in and were making hilarious faces like they were carved totems instead of people.

Casey smiled and glanced at us. She nodded her head that we should join in the chanting. We did, laughing loudly as we watched the girls and did our Ooga Ooga chants.

Tutu made her voice loud and dramatic, "The skies became fierce. The wind began to blooooow."

As Tutu said that, Emma and Sophia turned to each other, inhaled quickly, and blew air into each other's faces. They immediately started laughing.

I laughed and turned to look at Jessica. She blew air in my face. I laughed even more.

OOGA OOGA OOGA OOGA
OOGA OOGA OOGA OOGA

As Tutu began singing again, she slowed her rhythm, and made her voice sound very sad.

"The rain came down, for days and days,
the thunder it came too.
At last the man gave up his dream,
and left his big canoe."

When Tutu finished the last line, Emma and Sophia, with perfect comedic timing, both stopped dancing, shrugged their shoulders, made sad faces, and exclaimed, "Awwwww" really loudly. It was hilarious. We all started laughing.

As the "Awwwww" died away, Tutu smiled and began swaying and singing again. The girls resumed their dancing.

"He had not learned, the big big lesson,
most essential for all to know.
Put the most important things in first,
or on adventures you'll never go.

So remember this little story,
about the silly sailor who,
never went on his adventures,
because he could not pack his canoe.

Put what matters most in life,
in your canoe right at the start.
Or you'll have a life that is full of things,
but not adventures, which fill your heart."

⌒ Chapter 51

Casey began pounding like crazy on her drum again, to signal the end of the song. We joined her. The girls did more crazy dancing, including making hilarious faces at each other.

As we finished the song, I was laughing so hard I thought my stomach would hurt for a week. It seemed everyone else's would too, for they were laughing just as hard.

"I loved that," Jessica said finally. "That was so much fun." She looked at Emma and Sophia, "You two were amazing. How did you know all those movements so well?"

Emma smiled and danced about, "Tutu taught us. That's one of Sophia and my favorite songs. We practice it all the time with Tutu. Right, Sophia?"

Sophia laughed. "OOGA, OOGA," she said to Emma and began doing the funny movements of the dance.

Emma laughed, then pretended to be scared and started to run away. Sophia chased after her.

"Before the western cultures arrived, our Hawaiian tradition was to pass down information through stories and songs," Tutu said. "People learned that way." She looked toward the girls, "They will remember that song, and the lesson in it."

"I will too," Jessica said. "It seems so obvious now."

Tutu smiled, "Then it is a good story to learn and to share with others."

"And to write in my book of 'ahas!'," I said and got up. "Be right back."

I walked over to the café and went into the kitchen. My backpack was sitting on a shelf. I grabbed it and started to walk out. Then I stopped. I looked out through the order window into the café. Only a few lights were on, but I could still make it all out. The red booths, the long counter, the coat rack by the door....

My mind flashed back to my first visit. Sitting on the beach was fantastic. There was something magical about the inside of the café though. Especially now that it was nighttime. I smiled, grateful that for whatever reason, I had been given the chance to visit this place. Now revisit it.

"It has a special energy, doesn't it?"

I turned around. Casey was standing there, smiling. I hadn't heard her come in.

I nodded, then turned to look out at the café again. "Standing here reminds me of how much my life has changed," I finally replied. "Three questions and one night in a random café.... Where would I be had it not been for that night?" I shook my head, "Hard to imagine."

"You were ready," she replied. "And you acted in spirit with that readiness."

I turned and looked at her, "Somehow I just knew. I knew if I started filling my canoe with the things that mattered most to me, it would all work out. I didn't know *how* it would all work out. I just knew it would."

"And it has," she said.

I nodded, "To levels I couldn't have even imagined." I paused, "There's this leap of faith. You can plan, you can organize, you can think, you can talk to other people.... And then there comes a moment where you just have to step into the abyss. Only to realize it wasn't an abyss at all.

"The whole system, from the moment you arrived on the planet, was designed for you to move in that direction. You were being supported, guided, encouraged... the whole way. An intricate, beautifully designed game, organized for us to succeed, not fail."

I smiled, "I don't know why I'm telling you all this. I know you know."

She smiled and nodded, "Yes....I do.... Like everyone else though, there was a time when I didn't. There was a time when the fears and concerns and *have to's* and *musts*, and *need to's* and *can'ts* dominated my life. But once you've walked in alignment with your heart, and seen how it all works out, you let those go. That's what has been happening for you. What continues to happen for you. It's what will happen for Jessica too. When she leaps."

Casey looked at the backpack in my hand, "Getting your 'ahas!' book?"

I nodded, then reached inside and took it out.

"May I?" she asked, and extended her hand.

I gave it to her. She flipped to a random page. Then another. Then another. "Why do you work in between your travel years, John?" she asked, still holding the notebook. "Is it as fulfilling as the traveling?"

I laughed, "No. It's just the best solution I've come up with so far. Knowing I'll be back on the road within a year makes it easy to show up, do a great job, and not let it drag me down. I see it as an enabler for my traveling, so it has a purpose. A positive purpose.

"I know there's something better. As a matter of fact, Jessica and I were talking about that earlier today. I just haven't found what that better thing is yet." I gave her a quizzical look, "Why do you ask?"

"Mike and I were talking. About you, your 'ahas!'.... Do you have any plans for them?"

I shrugged, "Not really. I mean, I love them. I flip through my notebook almost every night before I go to sleep." I smiled, "They remind me about the abyss not really being an abyss."

"That's great energy to wrap yourself in before you go to bed," she said.

I nodded, "It is. I remember what I used to do instead—before my first visit here. I'd end my evening by watching the news. Or reading on the internet about the catastrophe of the day or some random celebrity story or sporting event.

"Then I'd turn off the lights and let my mind race for hours. Just replaying the problems of the day over and over. Or strategizing how to deal with the problems awaiting me the next day."

I smiled and shook my head a little, "And I wondered why I felt so tired all the time."

Casey listened quietly. "Well, like I mentioned, Mike and I were talking about you and your 'ahas!'," she said when I'd finished. "We think you should publish them."

I let that sink in. As it did, I no longer felt as sure of myself as I'd felt moments before. Doubts flashed through my mind. It's one thing to write something for yourself. Maybe share it with a few friends when they ask. It's a whole other reality to put those thoughts out into the world for other people to see and comment on. I mean, who was I to tell others about life's 'ahas!'?

Then, in that instant of fear and uncertainty, an image appeared in my mind. As if I had opened my 'ahas!' book and was looking right at one of the pages I'd created.

It was something I'd picked up while wandering around Costa Rica on one of my very first trips.

You can either live in faith, or you can live in fear, but not both.

Casey smiled, "You were correct when you wrote it, and it's still true now," she said. "And in addition to that...who are you not to?"

She was right. I knew what the truth was. I had just gotten done *explaining* how much I knew what the truth was. That the leap into the abyss wasn't a leap at all.

I shrugged.

Casey smiled again, "We'd like to be your first client, John. We'd like to gift your 'ahas!' book to customers at the café."

I looked at her in amazement, "Really?"

She nodded, "Really."

It was a shift. It had happened so fast. I'd felt the abyss. A giant place of unknown and fear. Then, just like that, the abyss was gone. With crystal clear precision, I could see the path in front of me.

"OK," I said. I nodded and smiled, "OK." Despite all my progress, I realized from that short experience, that I still had a lot to learn.

"We all do," Casey said. "That's why we're here."

◌◌ Chapter 52

Casey and I walked back out to the fire circle. Mike was playing on the ukelele and Tutu was teaching Jessica and the girls a new Hawaiian dance.

They were laughing and singing. It was great energy.

"Page fifty-six," Casey said to me.

I looked at her, confused.

Her eyes moved to my 'ahas!' book, which I was holding in my hand. I flipped it open. There had never been page numbers on the pages before. There were now. Neatly typed as if the notebook manufacturer had put them in right from the start.

I looked up at Casey. She shrugged, then winked. "Since you're going to publish them and all," she said.

I definitely still had a lot to learn. I flipped to page fifty-six.

You don't choose where you're born, but you do choose where you stay. You don't choose who you're born to, but you do choose who you stay around.

"Part of the adventure is coming to terms with what that means," Casey said. "Allowing yourself the freedom to make those choices and move on. Not just physically, but emotionally too." She nodded towards everyone, "That's part of what Jessica is realizing."

"I've learned that's what real freedom is," I replied. "The ability to not be constrained by something like where you were born, or the circumstances you were born into. Everyone I've met who has written their own story and defined their own way of living, has figured that out. And those are the people who seem to enjoy life the most."

"They've created their own playground," Casey added.

I nodded.

We arrived at the fire pit. Mike finished the song on the ukelele and the girls collapsed on the sand. They were still giggling and laughing.

Mike saw I was holding my 'ahas!' notebook. He looked at Casey, "Did you tell him?"

She nodded.

He looked at me. "What do you think? Can we be your first customer?"

I smiled and nodded, "Definitely."

He smiled back, "Great. Maybe somewhere down the line, those travels of yours won't require coming back to work for a year. You can fund the trips from the 'ahas!' books."

"I like that idea," I replied.

"My friend wrote a book and its been published in lots of different languages," Jessica said. "Now he goes and speaks to readers all over the world. He loves travel as much as you do. Now someone else pays for his traveling, which he really loves."

"There you go," Casey said. "Someone's out there doing it, why not you?"

"I'll introduce you to him," Jessica said.

"Ah, the universe at work," Tutu added. "Get clear on what you want, and it's like sending a homing beacon into the field of pure potential. In an instant, it all starts clicking into place."

◌ Chapter 53

My mind started to race. The fears and uncertainty from before were completely gone.

To get paid to travel around the world and speak to readers who were as into the 'ahas!' as I was.... That *would* be pretty amazing. Chills raced through me. It was the right idea. My body had just confirmed it. There was a great adventure waiting if I moved in this direction.

"May I look at your book?" Tutu asked.

"Sure," I replied and handed it to her.

She sat down in the sand and began to flip through it. I sat down too.

"How are you doing, Coconut?"

Mike had walked over to where Emma was sitting with Sophia. It was getting late, and after the food and dancing, the girls were starting to get tired. Emma reached her arms up toward Mike. He picked her up and held her to his chest. He kissed her on the top of the head.

"Is it about time to call it a night?"

She shook her head, "Not yet."

Mike sat down in the sand. Emma cuddled up in his lap with her head against his chest. Sophia made her way to Tutu and did the same.

Tutu smiled and stroked the top of Sophia's head. "Here is your book, John," she said and handed it to me. "Thank you for letting me see it."

"My pleasure."

"If you would like, I can help you," she added. "I have many friends here on the island, including some of the hotel owners. I think your book is very special. It's the kind of thing people would enjoy reading while sitting on the beach—when they have time to think. I don't know for sure, but perhaps some of those owners would purchase copies to give to their visitors too."

I couldn't believe it. "Really?"

She smiled, "Really. Contact me when you have copies ready and I will help you."

It was all happening so quickly. It surprised me and yet it shouldn't have. This was exactly what I'd discovered since first visiting the café. That when I locked onto something and knew it was my path, help was everywhere.

"Page seventy-one," Casey said and smiled.

I looked at her and flipped open the book to page seventy-one. I read the sentences out loud.

"When you look up at the sky on a starry night, what you can see is less than .00000005% of the stars in our galaxy. That is just our galaxy. There are at least one hundred and twenty five billion more galaxies out there. If a guiding presence can create all of that, surely the manifestation of your dream is well within it's capabilities. Ask for guidance and honor what you receive by acting upon it."

I smiled, "I wrote that in Africa. The star gazing there was like nowhere else I've ever been. You can clearly see the Milky Way with your naked eye. And with binoculars, you can look at individual stars and see them pulsing with blue, red, orange, and other colors.

"That was my second trip to Africa and when I was considering where to go, someone mentioned how unique and different Namibia is. I'd never heard of it. So I bought a Namibia travel book and when people would ask where I planned to go next, I'd mention I was thinking about Namibia.

"Not a week would go by without someone telling me they'd been there, or lived there, or had a friend who just got back from there.... It seemed like the universe was just watching, waiting for me to get clear. Once I did, then instantly all the connections appeared."

I smiled, "Thanks to all of you, it seems like the same thing is already happening for your idea of turning my 'ahas!' into a real book."

Jessica looked at Casey, "It's what you were explaining to me before, isn't it? This is what you meant."

Casey nodded, "Every moment, every second, we are in the middle of the field of pure potential. All our actions, whether we want them to or not, are sending signals. They are alerting the field of pure potential to what we want.

"In this case, John didn't just experience his 'ahas!'. They were important enough to him that he wrote them down. That sent a signal. He happily shared them with us when we asked if we could see them. That sent another signal. He responded positively to the idea of turning them into a book. Another signal.

"He responded positively again when you talked about your friend who wrote a book and gets paid to speak with readers. Yet another signal. Our offer to become customers, Tutu's offer to help...all additional signals. The universe sees the pattern start to emerge very quickly. And you get more of what you appear to be interested in."

"Take me, take me, take me again..." Tutu sang softly and smiled at Jessica and me.

"I get it," Jessica said. "If I'm unhappy with what I'm receiving, start sending a different signal. Start filling my canoe with what *truly* matters to me." She paused, "I really get it."

Tutu smiled, "Then you have just gotten one of the most important 'ahas!' there is."

◌ Chapter 54

Mike had picked up the 'ahas!' book and was flipping through it. He smiled.

"What's the significance of this one?" he asked and read it out loud.

"It's just a car."

I hesitated, then glanced at Jessica. I didn't say anything.

Mike smiled again, "Should I pick a different one?"

"It's just that...that...," I stammered.

I gave a quick sideways glance at Jessica. She was looking back at me.

"What is it?" Mike asked.

"He doesn't want to embarrass me," Jessica explained. "Go ahead," she said to me.

"I just..."

Jessica laughed, "You won't hurt my feelings. Go ahead."

I smiled, "OK. I have this friend. Every time I see him, he tells me he wishes he could do what I do. How he would love to go travel and see the world. Whenever I'm leaving on a trip, he always tells me he's going to meet up with me somewhere so I can teach him the ropes."

"But he never does?" Casey asked.

I shook my head, "Never. And when I've asked him about it, he tells me he can't get time off of work. Or there's some big project about to happen. It's always something. Which is fine. Except it really bothers him. He really does want to go."

"Can he take a break for a while?" Jessica asked.

I shook my head, "I've asked him that. The problem is, he spends almost everything he makes. He's in this routine where instead of putting some money aside and opening up space, he spends it the minute he has it. Then he feels like it's impossible to take any time off."

"Where does the car part come in?" Mike asked.

I was pretty sure he already knew the answer.

"Part of what keeps him locked into his job is his car. A few years back, he bought a brand new, very sleek, very stylish luxury car. It has every bell and whistle they offered at the dealership. Video screens to help you when you back up, heated seats, world wide GPS....

"It's a beauty. So are his payments. Add in insurance and repairs and every month he pays almost as much as I was paying in rent.

"Add that to his living expenses, and he feels like he can't possibly take time off. Especially to try something like I do, where it's for a whole year."

I shrugged, "Which is fine. I'm not judging him, or anyone else in that position. It's their life, their choice. I don't think he realizes though, how much that choice takes away his freedom to make other choices."

"Like traveling with you for a while," Tutu added.

I nodded, "Exactly. It would be one thing if he was totally into cars. But he isn't. Or if he had lots of opportunities to drive the car, which he doesn't. He lives in a city and takes a taxi everywhere. So the car just sits in a parking spot in a garage. Which he also has to pay for each month."

I shrugged again, "Spending is an impulse thing with him. He sees something, he wants it, he buys it. Then it ends up losing it's charm after a few days or months. So the benefit is pretty small, and the real cost is pretty big.

"To be honest, I think half the reason he owns the car is to show off. He's trying to make a statement to *someone* about *something*."

"To be a member of a club he doesn't really want to be a part of," Jessica said, and looked at Casey.

I nodded, "That's a great way to put it. I've never thought of it that way, but yes. I think in his case, there's a lot of truth to that. The last time I saw him, he was once again telling me how much he wished he was going to be joining me for my next travels. Which I knew wasn't going to happen."

I smiled, "At least as I was lamenting that, I had one of my 'ahas!'."

"Which was?" Jessica asked.

"Most of our cultural conditioning focuses on success or happiness being tied to how much money you have or things you own. As I've been traveling around the world, I've met a lot of different people. Some with tons of money, some with none.

"What they've taught me, is the currency which really matters isn't money. It's minutes. Being financially wealthy is neither bad nor good. It doesn't guarantee you're happy or sad. Neither does being poor. I'm amazed that whether I'm in the poorest regions of the world or the wealthiest, there are people who smile all the time and people who frown all the time.

"One of the common elements of the ones who smile all the time is their lifestyle. They've chosen to live in ways where they log lots of minutes each day doing things in alignment with their Purpose for Existing. In alignment with their heart."

"John, how much does your friend spend on his car?" Casey asked.

"Almost nine hundred dollars a month. Plus another two hundred dollars per month for parking. All for a car he never uses. Which means he doesn't get many quality minutes in exchange for his money.

"If he'd have saved that much money every month for a year and a half, he could have traveled the world with me—for a *whole year*! And that would have gotten him a lot of quality minutes."

I shrugged, "So I wrote that note in my book to remind myself to spend in alignment with the life I really want to live." I looked at Jessica, "Sorry, I don't mean to offend you. I have another friend who really *is* into cars. He drives a 1968 classic convertible and for him, it's a great use of his money. He loves that car. Drives it everywhere. He also loves meeting people, and the car is a fantastic conversation starter everywhere he goes. For him, his car choice makes perfect sense."

Jessica smiled, "It's OK. You're not offending me. Making me think, yes. But not offending me."

"The truth is, it's not even about cars," I said. "The point of the note in my 'ahas!' book is to remind myself to spend in alignment with the life I really want. For me, that's travel and adventure. For another person, it might be something totally different."

I nodded toward Casey and smiled, "One of my greatest take-aways from my first visit to the café was on this exact topic."

"Which was?" Jessica asked.

"Make sure that something has meaning because *you* determine it has meaning. Not because someone else convinces you it does."

"I like that," Jessica said.

I nodded, "When I left here last time, I no longer looked at my money the same way. It was a pretty eye opening experience. I realized quite a bit of my spending was out of synch with what I really wanted to experience in life."

I smiled, "By most people's standards, my work years aren't very glamorous. I don't go out a ton, and I don't buy much. And compared to a one week luxury vacation, my year-long travels aren't flashy."

I smiled again, "But in the context of what really matters to *me*...my travel years *are* extraordinary. Different countries, different cultures, interesting people, new adventures every day.... The work years may be a little sparse, but in the travel years, I log a huge amount of incredible minutes."

ও Chapter 55

Tutu stroked Sophia's hair. She was sound asleep with her head in Tutu's lap.

"I have a story for you, Jessica. Would you like to hear it? I believe you will find a connection in it for why you have come upon the café today."

"I'd love to hear it," Jessica replied.

Tutu smiled and stroked Sophia's hair again, "Alright then. And after that it will be time to take this little one home to bed."

Tutu closed her eyes for a moment and then began, "Have you ever seen a foggy morning, Jessica? Where the fog was so thick you could barely see through it?"

Jessica nodded.

"This story is about a fog such as that. Picture a big old beautiful house, with a wide front porch. Surrounding the house is a spacious yard, which is then surrounded by thick forest. There is a path which leads from the porch, across the yard, and off into the forest. And sitting on the porch, overlooking that path, is a rocking chair."

Tutu looked at Jessica, "Can you envision all of that?"

Jessica nodded again.

"In my experience," Tutu continued, "for most people, life is like sitting in that rocking chair. Only when they look out beyond the porch railing, they don't see the yard or the trees. What they see is that thick fog. It is a fog comprised of all the things other people are trying to get them to do, see, and believe. A fog which contains all their self doubts, and fears, and uncertainties. Plus all the negative conditioning which they have accepted over the course of their life.

"And they sit on the porch, rocking in that chair. As they do, they think to themselves that if that fog would part for just five minutes, and they could see the path which leads to the life they really want...they would get up off that chair, march down those steps, and go live that life.

"Then one day, they read an inspirational story, or hear about someone who just fulfilled a long-held dream. As if by magic, for five minutes the fog parts and they can clearly see the path to the life they really want to live. It is beautiful and brilliant, and calls to them. For five minutes, they think of getting up and starting down that path. They imagine the adventures they would have and the joy they would experience.

"But then the five minutes pass, and the fog closes in again. So they shift back in their chair...and they rock. Back and forth.

"Over time, they think to themselves that if for just one *hour* that fog would part, and they could see the life they really want...they would get up off their chair, march down those steps, and go live that life.

"Then one day, they see a particularly inspiring movie, or listen to someone's incredible real life story. It's a message which is just perfect for them. As if the director could see inside their mind, or the person was speaking directly to them. And for the next hour, the fog parts and they can clearly see the path to the life they really want.

"It is beautiful and brilliant, and calls to them. For that whole hour they think of getting up and starting down the path. They imagine the adventures they would have and the joy they would experience.

"But then the hour ends, and the fog closes in again. So they shift to the back of their chair...and they rock. Back and forth.

"Over time, they think to themselves that if for just twenty-four hours that fog would part, and they could see the life they really want, they would get up off their chair, march down those steps, and go live that life.

"Then one day they hear that a friend of theirs has died. A good person. Someone who treated others well. Someone who was too bright of a light to have died so young. And for the next twenty-four hours, the fog parts and they have a clarity like they have never had before.

"They see the path to the life they really want and it calls to them with an intensity greater than it ever has before. It is beautiful and brilliant. They see all the reasons in the world why they should walk it, and see the fallacy in all their old reasons why they couldn't. For those twenty-four hours they feel an urgency to move, to start, to begin....

"But then the day ends, and the fog closes in again. So they shift back in their chair...and they rock. Back and forth.

"Then one morning, they look out, and there is no fog anymore. They wait for an hour, but the fog does not appear.

"A day passes, then two days and still the fog is nowhere to be found. As they look out across the porch, they can clearly see the path to the life they really want.

"It is beautiful and brilliant, and calls to them. They imagine the adventures they would have and the joy they would experience if they were to only walk it. Eventually, they can bear it no more. Today is the day.

"They get up from their chair, and try to take a step.... Only to realize...they are no longer able to walk."

I looked at Jessica. She was crying.

"You are young, Jessica," Tutu began softly. "You are smart. You are talented. There are many adventures just waiting for you. But you must let go of the fog."

"There are days when it is so thick," Jessica said quietly through the tears. "Today was *so* clear. Spending time with all of you has taken all the fog away."

She paused, "But what happens when it closes in again? When I can't see the path anymore?"

"You get up and start walking anyway," Tutu replied. "The path is always there, waiting for you to see it. Often it only requires that first step into the unknown."

"I'm not sure," Jessica said.

Tutu let the silence hang in the air for a moment. "In the most dense fog you can imagine, how far can you see, Jessica?"

Jessica hesitated.

Tutu nodded at her.

"Ten feet."

"And if you stay on that porch, you will always see the same ten feet," Tutu replied.

She let the silence fill the air again. "If you get up and take just one step. A single step. How far can you see?"

Jessica shrugged, as if she didn't understand the significance, "Ten feet."

"Yes. But it is not the same ten feet."

Jessica was silent.

"Come here, child," Tutu said to her.

Like a little girl, Jessica crawled through the sand until she was next to Tutu. She put her forehead to Tutu's and cried. She cried until there were no tears left.

Tutu waited patiently, comforting Jessica, like a loving mother would her child. When Jessica stopped crying, Tutu placed her hands on Jessica's face and looked at her. "When you took that first step today, the first nine feet were the same as they have always been. The last one though was different. It was new. And it was there that the universe had placed the start of your path."

Jessica smiled. She wiped the tears from her cheeks. "Why didn't it just place it closer?" she said and laughed through the tears.

Tutu shook her head a little and smiled too, "Because that is not how it works."

Chapter 56

Casey, Jessica and I cleaned up the luau items and carried them to the kitchen. Mike and Tutu stayed outside, holding Emma and Sophia.

"I can take care of these," I said and started putting water into the sink to wash the dishes.

Casey smiled, "That's OK, John. You've been a big help today. I'll take care of finishing up for tonight."

"Are you sure?" I asked.

She nodded and smiled, "I'm sure."

Jessica put down the things she was carrying. "I'm happy to help," she said.

Casey shook her head a little and smiled again, "Thanks, Jessica. I've got it though. Really."

Jessica looked out through the order window into the café. Her business suit, high heels, and purse were sitting in the booth where she had first sat down that morning. "It seems like a million years ago," she said hesitantly. "A million lifetimes ago."

She looked back at Casey. "It will be OK," Casey said. "That was before you knew. This is after."

There was a menu sitting on one of the kitchen counters. Jessica picked it up and turned it over.

Why are you here?
Are you playing in your playground?
Do you have MPO?

She looked at Casey, "The last question. We never talked about it."

Casey smiled, "Who were you today?"

"What do you mean?"

"Who were you today?"

Jessica thought for a minute, "When I arrived I was a business woman." She smiled sheepishly, "A pretty high strung business woman. Then I was a customer in a very unusual café." She paused, "On the swings I was a little girl again. Out there," she nodded toward the ocean, "I was a surfer, for the first time ever in my life."

"And then?" Casey asked.

Jessica laughed, "I was a drummer, and a dancer, and a learner...."

"And out of all of those, which one was really *you*?" Casey asked.

Jessica looked at her, "Before today I would have said just the first one." She paused, "But it would have been a lie. They are all me."

Casey smiled, "Then you are very fortunate. You have MPO. Multiple Personality Order. You understand that life is multi-faceted. And that *you* are multi-faceted too. You embrace the fact that at any given moment you may be a drummer, a surfer, a learner, a little girl, or any of the other personalities which make you uniquely you. You also embrace the unique energies and emotions which accompany that.

"You give yourself the gift of being all the personalities you are. Of keeping open all the rides in your playground which make you smile, bring you joy, and make you feel authentically you."

Casey smiled again, "Sometimes it only takes a small connection to another part of our personality to enable all of who we are to bloom. We had a customer come in one time who had stopped singing many years earlier. It had been one of her favorite parts of her playground. After her stay here, she started singing again. Just one night a week for an hour with a local choir.

"She said that one hour of singing made her a better mom, a better wife, a better employee...a better person. It changed everything."

"Hearing you say that makes me feel so free," Jessica said. "It's like hearing something I've always believed was true, but didn't trust myself to allow. That is me. The surfer, the drummer, the little girl.... And all the emotions that come with them. I am all those things."

"And probably a hundred more," Casey said and smiled. She held out her arms. Jessica hugged her tightly.

"Thank you," Jessica said.

"You're welcome."

When the two parted, Jessica turned to me, "Thank you too, John. This morning I was about to leave when you came over to the table and talked to me. If you hadn't done that, I never would have gotten to experience all I did today."

This time it was she who held out her arms. We hugged.

"I'm glad you were here today," I said. "And I'm glad I could help."

⌒⌒ Chapter 57

Tutu and Mike came into the kitchen. They were carrying the girls, who were still sleeping.

Casey held out her arms and Tutu passed Sophia to her. Sophia tucked up against Casey's shoulder.

"We wanted to say aloha," Tutu said. She smiled, "I think I will have to say it for Sophia too."

Jessica hugged Tutu, "Aloha. And mahalo. Thank you for all you have taught me tonight."

"Why don't we surf together next week," Tutu said. "A little girl time, you and me."

Jessica's face lit up even brighter than it had been. "Really? I would love that."

"Me too."

Tutu turned to me and gave me a hug, "Aloha, John. It has been a great pleasure. I will wait anxiously for your 'ahas!' book. Then I will help you share it around the island."

"It has been a great pleasure for me too," I replied. "And thank you for your offer to help. I will take you up on it."

Tutu hugged Casey and Mike and said her good-byes to them. Casey passed Sophia back to her.

"Would you like me to walk the two of you home?" Casey asked.

Tutu shook her head, "That is very kind of you, Casey but not necessary." She smiled, "I have been walking the path to this magical spot since I was a little girl. We'll be fine."

And then she was gone. Out the door and on her way.

Jessica glanced out to the front of the café. "I'm going to go freshen up and grab my things," she said.

I watched her walk out to the table where her phone and other items were.

"You helped her a lot today, John," Casey said. "She looks like a new person compared to this morning."

"I remember what that feels like," I said, and glanced

from Casey to Mike. "How much someone can change from spending a little time at this place, with the two of you."

Mike smiled and adjusted his hold on Emma, "It was good to see you again, John." He extended his hand.

I shook it and smiled back, "Same here. Thanks for all the conversations."

He nodded, "Casey, do you mind taking things from here? I'll get this little one off to bed."

She nodded, "Happy to."

"Aloha, John," Mike said and he turned and headed out the back door.

"Aloha, Mike," I replied.

It was quiet now.

"Let's head out to the front," Casey said.

We walked out of the kitchen and into the front area of the café. As we walked past them, I ran my hand over the chrome sides of the counter and the tops of the soda fountain stools. A sense of sadness washed over me.

"You'll be back," Casey said. "A lot sooner than you think."

I looked at her, "If I bike here tomorrow will this place be here?"

She smiled, "That depends on a million different things, John."

I felt sad again.

She put her hand on my shoulder, "When your book of 'ahas!' is done, keep your eyes open. We've got an order to pick up from you."

I nodded.

Just then, Jessica came out from the restrooms and walked towards us. She had changed out of her bathing suit and was back wearing her business clothes. Her hair was pinned up in the same fashion as when she'd first arrived at the café, and she was wearing her high heels. As she came closer, her phone rang. She stopped and reached into her purse.

I looked at Casey. She shrugged.

Jessica lifted her phone out of her purse. She'd missed the call. "Isn't that the strangest thing," she said while looking at the phone. "Now there's plenty of signal. And lots of messages." She began playing with the phone, scrolling through the messages. Her face became intense and serious.

I glanced at Casey again.

"It's pretty late, John," Casey said. "You've got your

bike, right? Are you going to be OK going home from here?"

I nodded, "It's pretty dark out on these roads, but I'll take it slow. I'll be fine."

I honestly wasn't exactly sure how to get back home. But I figured I could sort it out.

"I'll drive you."

It was Jessica. She was holding her phone in her hand, but looking at me.

"I can drive you home."

I looked at her, standing there in her business suit and high heels, "That's OK, Jessica. My bike isn't too clean after the long ride I took this morning before I got here. Plus, your car isn't exactly designed for hauling bikes. I don't want to get it all messed up...."

Jessica looked at Casey and I and smiled. The intensity and seriousness of moments ago were gone from her face. Her smile was once again that same, wide open, beautiful energy smile she'd had since walking back from the swings earlier in the day. She turned off her phone and threw it in her purse.

"What is it?" I asked.

"It's just a car," she said, and her smile grew even more bright. "It's just a car."

Thank you very much for visiting *The Why Café*.

We have a gift for you!

You can download for free our new e-book titled- "1001 Inspirational Quotes" by visiting www.whycafe.com/quotebook

It is fully searchable, and fully inspirational!

You can also find other resources to help you discover and live *your* Purpose for Existing and Big Five for Life at:

www.whycafe.com

These include in person and online courses available throughout the year, as well as ...
John's book of "Ahas!".

Thanks, and enjoy your book of inspiring quotes!

ꙮ About the Author

Following a life changing event when he was thirty-three years old, John was inspired to sit down and tell the story of *The Why Café*. He had no previous experience or academic training as a writer.

Within a year after its release, word of mouth support from readers had spread the book across the globe—inspiring people on every continent, including Antarctica. It went on to become a #1 Best Seller, and has been translated into more than twenty-five languages.

John has since written other books, including *Life Safari*, *The Big Five for Life*, and now, *Return to The Why Café*. He coauthored the book *How to be Rich and Happy*.

Through his writings and appearances on television and radio, John's simple yet thought provoking messages have inspired millions to live life on their terms. In response to his endeavors, he has been honored alongside Oprah Winfrey, Wayne Dyer, and Deepak Chopra as one of the one hundred most inspirational thought leaders in the field of leadership and personal development. All of this continues to humble and amaze him.

When he isn't writing, he is often out traveling the world with his family.

To learn more about John, or to inquire about his availability as a speaker, please visit;

www.whycafe.com

11/17 Amazon 14.97 ✓